HERSTORY OF ECONOMICS

THE EVOLUTION OF WOMEN IN THE ECONOMIC WORLD

MUSTAFA NABI SHAH
MOHAMMAD HASAN

Made with ♥ on the Notion Press Platform
www.notionpress.com

To my Family & Friends

Contents

Foreword

The book titled HerStory of Economics: The Evolution of Women in the Economic World is a very well-researched book written by Mr.Mustafa Nabi Shah. It contains a chapter on every aspect of women and their relationship with the economy. The transition in the role of women in the economy from the ancient to the modern period is aptly depicted by the author. Particularly the description by the author of the profound impact of industrialization on women's lives and the role of women in industries is commendable.

The great merit of this book is that here a reader will study the various facets of women from hunters/gatherers to agricultural workers to those working in modern industries, this evolution is beautifully described by the author. It discusses the cultural barriers to women's economic participation which has traditionally created a lot of constraints on women's role in the decision-making process that has ultimately affected the economic aspects also at micro as well as at macro levels. The inheritance laws severely curtail the women's power which does hurt their confidence levels. The book also covered critical issues such as the challenges faced by women in rural as well as urban areas, gender inequalities and formal education which significantly affected their economic participation and contribution to the economic growth process. Further, even after the transition and the incorporation of women in industries, women including child labour had to face challenges related to the working environment, this aspect is also examined in this book. The emergence of female-dominated industries where the majority of workers were female is nicely framed by the author.

A very central topic of women's economic rights is also covered in this book which is very important to understand as it determines the extent of participation of women in the economic development process of that country.

The book has covered another important turning point in the history of the world which was World War II, which brought a significant transition in the role of women in society and their participation in economic activities, particularly from employment perspectives. Mr. Mustafa Nabi Shah has further extended his analysis by incorporating the role of women in modern corporate houses, the gender pay gap, financial insecurities, health inequalities, etc., which is very important to understand in the present scenario of the industrialized world. Above all, the book finally looks into the role of women in economics, such as entrepreneurial roles. However, it has been challenged by various constraints like lack of access to financial resources, digital divide, etc., which makes it a challenging task for modern-day women. There is a need to pay attention in this direction if we want to increase the female participation rate in economic activities.

The materials incorporated in this book are not easily available. The author deserves appreciation for his dedication in writing this book and bringing most of the facets of women under one roof. There are not many books on women that have extensive coverage of numerous aspects of women, as this book has admirably incorporated. I compliment Mr. Mustafa Nabi Shah for his diligent efforts that have taken the shape of this captivating book. I feel that every reader of this book would like to have a copy of this book on their bookshelf. It is worth reading for all of us, particularly for those who are working on women-related issues. The writing skills of Mr. Mustafa Nabi Shah are outstanding, and his understanding of the concern aspect is admirable. My best wishes are with the young writer of this brilliant piece of work.

Prof. Shehroz A. Rizvi
Professor & Chairman
Department of Economics
Aligarh Muslim University, Aligarh

Preface

In the annals of history, the contributions of women to economic progress have often been overlooked or minimized. This book seeks to rectify this oversight, offering a comprehensive exploration of women's roles in the economy, from ancient civilizations to the modern digital age. Through a meticulous examination of historical contexts, global movements, and contemporary challenges, this work illuminates the multifaceted ways in which women have shaped and continue to shape economic landscapes across the globe.

The narrative woven within these pages challenges traditional notions of women's economic participation, revealing their agency, resilience, and innovation in the face of systemic barriers. From the fields of ancient agricultural societies to the factories of the Industrial Revolution, from the boardrooms of Fortune 500 companies to the bustling marketplaces of the Global South, women have consistently demonstrated their economic prowess and their capacity to drive change.

This book is not just a historical account; it is a call to action. By understanding the historical and contemporary challenges women face, we can chart a path toward a more equitable and inclusive economic future. The stories of women entrepreneurs, activists, and leaders featured in this work serve as an inspiration, reminding us that the pursuit of economic empowerment is not just a matter of individual ambition but a collective endeavor that benefits us all.

As we navigate the complexities of the 21st-century economy, the insights offered in this book are more relevant than ever. The digital revolution, globalization, and the ongoing struggle for gender equality present both challenges and opportunities for women's economic advancement. By embracing the lessons of the past and the possibilities of the future, we can create a world where women's economic contributions are fully recognized, valued, and celebrated.

CHAPTER I

Historical Context of Women's Roles in Ancient Economies

The narrative of women's economic roles in ancient societies has often been obscured by traditional interpretations that emphasize male-dominated activities like hunting and warfare. However, a growing body of archaeological evidence, coupled with fresh perspectives from anthropology and feminist studies, is challenging these conventional views. By examining the historical context of women's con
Contributions, we can uncover a more nuanced and comprehensive understanding of their diverse and often crucial roles in the economic life of their communities.

Women's Roles in Hunter-Gatherer Societies

In the earliest human societies, characterized by hunting and gathering, women played an active and indispensable role in ensuring the survival and prosperity of their groups. Far from being passive participants relegated to the domestic sphere, women were skilled foragers, their intimate knowledge of plant resources and gathering techniques often providing a substantial portion, if not the majority, of the community's caloric intake (Fedurek et al., 2020). Anthropological studies of contemporary hunter-gatherer groups like the Hadza of Tanzania, for instance, reveal that women's gathering efforts can, at times, surpass the caloric contributions of male hunters (Hansen et al., 2015). This challenges the long-held assumption of male dominance in subsistence activities and underscores the economic significance of women's labor in these egalitarian societies.

Beyond gathering, women in hunter-gatherer societies likely participated in a wide array of other essential tasks, contributing to the overall well-being of their communities. These tasks could include toolmaking, shelter construction, hide processing, and childcare. The division of labor was often fluid and adaptable, with individuals taking on different roles depending on the specific needs of the group and the availability of resources. For example, while men might primarily engage in hunting during certain seasons or when animal resources were plentiful, women's gathering activities would become more crucial during periods of scarcity or when plant resources were abundant (Anderson et al., 2023).

This flexible division of labor fostered a sense of interdependence and mutual respect within hunter-gatherer communities. Both men's and women's contributions were valued and recognized as essential for survival, leading to a relatively egalitarian social structure where women enjoyed a degree of autonomy and decision-making power not always seen in later, more stratified societies. This is exemplified by the fact that women in some hunter-gatherer groups actively participated in group discussions and decision-making processes, demonstrating their agency and influence within their communities.

Division of Labor in Ancient Civilizations

The transition from hunting and gathering to agriculture marked a significant turning point in human history, ushering in profound changes in social organization, economic systems, and gender roles. While evidence suggests that early agricultural societies may have initially maintained some of the flexibility in labor divisions characteristic of hunter-gatherer groups, with women continuing to participate in various activities beyond the domestic sphere (Fedurek et al., 2020), the increasing complexity of these societies and the growing emphasis on agricultural production gradually led to more defined and often more rigid gender roles (Hansen et al., 2015).

In agricultural communities like the Kaguru of East Africa, while both men and women worked the land, certain tasks like herding and roof thatching were designated as male activities (Redd, 1998). This separation of roles, coupled with land tenure systems that often favored men and restricted women's ownership of large plots, contributed to a growing disparity in economic power and status between the genders (Hansen et al., 2015). As societies further developed and specialized crafts and trades emerged, this division of labor intensified, with women increasingly confined to activities within the household or those considered less skilled or valuable (Redd, 1998).

This shift towards more defined gender roles and the devaluation of women's labor had far-reaching consequences. It not only limited women's economic opportunities but also contributed to their increasing dependence on men and their exclusion from decision-making processes.

While women continued to play essential roles in food processing, childcare, and other domestic tasks, their contributions were often overshadowed by those of men, who were seen as the primary providers and decision-makers within their communities.

Gender Roles in Pre-Industrial Societies

The shift from hunter-gatherer lifestyles to settled agricultural communities marked a pivotal turning point in human history, bringing about profound transformations in social structures, economic systems, and gender roles. As societies embraced agriculture as their primary means of subsistence, women's roles and contributions underwent a complex and often paradoxical evolution (Redd, 1998). While they remained vital to the economic well-being of their communities, their labor was increasingly confined to specific spheres and often undervalued compared to the activities of men.

Agricultural Societies and Women's Labor

In pre-industrial agricultural societies, women's labor was indispensable for the success of both household and community economies. They toiled tirelessly in the fields, planting, weeding, harvesting, and processing crops. Their knowledge of plant cultivation and their expertise in various agricultural tasks were essential for ensuring food security and the overall prosperity of their communities (Hansen et al., 2015).

Despite their crucial contributions, the cultural narratives of these societies often downplayed the significance of women's agricultural labor. In many cultures, the physically demanding tasks performed by men, such as plowing and clearing land, were given greater prominence and prestige. For example, among the Hadza, hunting was celebrated as a heroic and masculine activity, while women's gathering efforts were often seen as secondary or supplementary (Redd, 1998). This societal bias towards valuing male-dominated activities perpetuated a perception of women's labor as less important, even though it was equally essential for the survival and well-being of the community.

Furthermore, the introduction of new agricultural technologies and practices often led to a further marginalization of women's labor. For instance, the adoption of cereal-based agriculture in many societies reduced the need for women's involvement in fieldwork, as these crops required less intensive labor compared to other types of cultivation (Hansen et al., 2015). This shift further confined women to the domestic sphere and reinforced the gendered division of labor.

Domestic Responsibilities and Economic Value

The domestic sphere remained a central arena for women's economic contributions in pre-industrial societies. Women were responsible for a multitude of tasks that were essential for the functioning of households and, by extension, the entire community (Redd, 1998). These tasks included cooking, cleaning, childcare, textile production, and the preservation of food. While often overlooked or dismissed as merely "women's work," these activities were fundamental for the well-being and survival of families and played a crucial role in the overall economy (Fedurek et al., 2020).

The economic value of domestic labor, however, was rarely acknowledged or quantified in traditional economic models. Unlike the more visible and quantifiable products of men's labor, such as crops or livestock, the contributions of women within the household were often seen as intangible and therefore less valuable. This devaluation of domestic labor further entrenched women's economic disadvantage and perpetuated the notion that their work was less important than that of men (Anderson et al., 2023).

Moreover, the domestic sphere was often intertwined with the agricultural economy. Women's knowledge of food processing and preservation techniques was crucial for ensuring the long-term viability of agricultural produce. Their skills in textile production contributed to the household economy and, in some cases, could be traded or sold for additional income. The interconnectedness of domestic and agricultural labor highlights the multifaceted nature of women's economic contributions in pre-industrial societies.

Legal and Cultural Barriers to Women's Economic Participation

While the essential role of women's labor in pre-industrial societies is undeniable, their economic participation was often severely curtailed by a complex interplay of legal and cultural constraints. These barriers, deeply entrenched in societal norms and reinforced by legal frameworks, systematically limited women's access to resources, control over their own labor, and overall economic agency. The historical context reveals a disheartening pattern of marginalization and inequality that persisted for centuries, hindering women's potential to fully contribute to and benefit from the economic systems of their communities.

Property Rights and Inheritance Laws

One of the most formidable legal barriers to women's economic empowerment was the unequal distribution of property rights and inheritance laws. In a vast majority of pre-industrial societies, women were systematically denied the right to own or inherit property independently. This meant that their access to land, livestock, and other essential resources was often contingent upon their relationships with male relatives, be it fathers, husbands, or brothers (Hansen et al., 2015).

This lack of property rights not only curtailed women's economic independence but also perpetuated a cycle of dependency on men, reinforcing their subordinate social status and limiting their ability to make autonomous decisions about their lives.

Across different cultures and regions, the specifics of these legal restrictions varied. In some societies, women were completely barred from owning any property, while in others, they might have had limited rights to certain types of assets, such as personal belongings or dowry items. However, the overarching principle remained the same: women's access to economic resources was mediated through men, rendering them vulnerable to exploitation and control. For instance, among the Kaguru of East Africa, land tenure systems were structured in such a way that women were rarely allowed to own large plots of land in their own right (Redd, 1998).

This effectively excluded them from participating in agricultural production on a larger scale and denied them the social and economic prestige associated with land ownership.

Inheritance laws further exacerbated this inequality. In many ancient civilizations, primogeniture, the practice of passing down property and titles to the eldest son, was the norm (Fedurek et al., 2020).

This left women with little or no inheritance, forcing them to rely on their families or husbands for economic support. Even in cases where women were allowed to inherit, their shares were often smaller than those of their male siblings, further entrenching gender disparities in wealth and economic power.

Gender Norms and Societal Expectations

Beyond the legal arena, deeply ingrained cultural norms and societal expectations created a formidable barrier to women's economic participation. In most pre-industrial societies, women were socialized from a young age to prioritize their roles as wives and mothers, dedicating their time and energy to domestic tasks and child-rearing (Anderson et al., 2023). While these responsibilities were undoubtedly important for the well-being of families and communities, they often came at the expense of women's ability to engage in economic activities outside the household.

Societal expectations also dictated the types of work considered appropriate for women. In many cultures, women were relegated to specific occupations that were deemed "feminine" or less physically demanding. These occupations often included weaving, pottery making, food processing, and certain agricultural tasks like weeding and harvesting (Redd, 1998). While essential for the functioning of the household and community, these occupations were often less prestigious and less remunerative than those typically performed by men, further reinforcing the economic disparities between genders.

Moreover, women's mobility and freedom of movement were often severely restricted by societal norms. In some cultures, women were expected to remain within the confines of their homes or villages, limiting their ability to participate in trade, markets, or other economic activities that required travel or interaction with the wider world (Anderson et al., 2023). This confinement not only hindered their access to economic opportunities but also reinforced their isolation and dependence on men.

The Impact of Religion and Philosophy on Economic Exclusion

The marginalization of women in pre-industrial economies was not merely a product of legal and cultural constraints; it was also deeply intertwined with prevailing religious and philosophical beliefs. These systems of thought, often codified in sacred texts and scholarly treatises, frequently served to justify and reinforce the existing gender hierarchies, further solidifying women's economic exclusion. By examining the specific doctrines and arguments put forth by various religions and philosophies, we can gain a deeper understanding of how these ideological frameworks contributed to the systemic denial of women's economic rights and opportunities.

Religious Doctrines on Women's Roles

In many pre-industrial societies, religion played a pivotal role in shaping social norms and values, including those related to gender roles and economic participation. Religious texts and interpretations often emphasized women's domestic responsibilities and subservience to men, portraying these roles as divinely ordained and essential for maintaining social order (Hansen et al., 2015). This emphasis on women's domesticity frequently stemmed from a belief in their inherent inferiority to men, both physically and intellectually. Many religious doctrines assigned specific duties to women based on these perceived limitations, restricting their participation in public life and economic activities beyond the household.

For example, in ancient Greece, the works of prominent philosophers like Aristotle reinforced the notion of women's natural inferiority and their suitability for domestic life. Aristotle argued that women were "incomplete" or "mutilated" males, lacking the rational capacity and moral fortitude required for public and political participation (Anderson et al., 2023). This philosophical perspective, while not universally accepted, had a profound influence on societal attitudes towards women and their economic roles. It provided intellectual justification for excluding women from economic activities beyond the household and reinforced the notion that their primary purpose was to serve as wives and mothers.

Similarly, in ancient India, the Laws of Manu, a Hindu legal text, prescribed strict gender roles and limited women's access to education and economic opportunities. Women were expected to be obedient to their fathers, husbands, and sons, and their primary duty was to bear and raise children (Fedurek et al., 2020). The Laws of Manu even went so far as to state that "a woman must never seek independence," further emphasizing the patriarchal nature of these religious doctrines and their role in perpetuating women's economic dependence.

Philosophical Justifications for Economic Exclusion

Philosophical traditions also played a role in perpetuating the economic exclusion of women. In many ancient societies, philosophical arguments were used to rationalize the existing gender hierarchies and justify the unequal distribution of resources and opportunities. These arguments often drew upon the prevailing cultural norms and the perceived "natural" differences between men and women to reinforce the idea that women were inherently unsuited for certain roles or activities.

For instance, in ancient China, Confucian philosophy emphasized the importance of maintaining social order and adhering to traditional gender roles. Women were expected to be virtuous, submissive, and devoted to their families, while men were expected to be the leaders and providers (Redd, 1998). This philosophical framework not only limited women's access to education and economic opportunities but also reinforced the notion that their primary value lay in their ability to fulfill their domestic duties.

In ancient Greece, the concept of "separate spheres" was prevalent, with the public sphere reserved for men and the private sphere for women (Anderson et al., 2023). This division was justified by philosophical arguments that emphasized women's supposed emotional nature and their lack of rationality, which were deemed essential for participation in public life and economic activities.

While not all ancient religions and philosophies were inherently discriminatory, the dominant ideologies in many pre-industrial societies often served to justify and perpetuate the economic exclusion of women. These beliefs, deeply embedded in cultural norms and social structures, created a formidable barrier to women's economic empowerment, hindering their potential to fully contribute to and benefit from the economic systems of their communities.

CHAPTER II

THE INDUSTRIAL REVOLUTION AND WOMEN'S LABOR

Shift from Agrarian to Industrial Economies

The transition from agrarian to industrial economies marked a profound transformation in labor and family life, with significant implications for women. As economies shifted from agriculture-based to industry-based, traditional roles and working conditions for women underwent dramatic changes.

Impact on Traditional Women's Work

Before industrialization, women's work was largely centered around domestic and community-based activities that were integral to the household economy. In agrarian societies, women were involved in tasks such as farming, textile production, and food processing, which were crucial for the survival and economic stability of their families. For example, in rural areas, women's labor included activities like spinning, weaving, and preparing food, which were not only vital for household consumption but also for local markets (Cohen, n.d.). These activities allowed women to contribute economically while remaining within the sphere of their homes.

With the onset of industrialization, many of these traditional roles were altered or displaced. The advent of machinery and the factory system meant that tasks previously performed at home were now conducted in centralized locations. Technologies such as the spinning jenny and power loom revolutionized textile production, which had previously been a significant part of women's home-based work (Cowan, 1976). As production moved to factories, women who had once worked in the domestic sphere found themselves transitioning to new roles in industrial settings. This shift often led to a reduction in the visibility and perceived value of their labor, as factory work was viewed as more modern and essential compared to traditional home-based tasks (Foster & Clark, 2018).

The decline of home-based production not only affected women's economic roles but also altered the structure of their work. The factory system introduced a division between work and home, where previously there had been a more integrated approach. This transition often resulted in women's skills being undervalued and their contributions to the household economy being diminished, as the significance of home-based tasks became less apparent in the new industrial context (Stanfors & Goldscheider, 2017).

Urbanization and Changes in Family Structure

The rise of industrial economies also led to rapid urbanization, with many families moving from rural areas to cities in search of better economic opportunities. This migration had a profound impact on family structure and dynamics. In agrarian societies, family units were often extended, with multiple generations living together and contributing to the household economy. This extended family model provided a support network that facilitated the management of both domestic responsibilities and economic activities (Cohen, n.d.).

In contrast, urban environments promoted the nuclear family structure, where households typically consisted of parents and their children. This shift had significant implications for women, who now had to manage their domestic responsibilities with fewer family members available to share the load (Stanfors & Goldscheider, 2017). Urban living also brought about new economic pressures, as many women were compelled to enter the workforce to help support their families. This added responsibility often resulted in a dual burden of paid labor and domestic work, leading to increased stress and a reevaluation of traditional gender roles (Cowan, 1976).

Moreover, the separation of work and home in urban settings reinforced gendered divisions, where men were increasingly associated with the public sphere of work and women with domestic duties. Despite the growing necessity for women to contribute economically, societal expectations often confined them to the private sphere of home and family, reflecting a persistent gender disparity (Foster & Clark, 2018).

The lack of extended family support in urban settings also meant that women faced greater challenges in balancing work and home responsibilities. The shift from agrarian to industrial economies thus not only altered women's roles in the workforce but also transformed family dynamics, leading to new social and economic pressures (Stanfors & Goldscheider, 2017).

Women in Factories: Conditions and Challenges

As women transitioned to factory work, they encountered new working environments that brought both opportunities and significant challenges. Factories became a central feature of industrial economies, employing large numbers of women, but the conditions in these workplaces were often harsh and exploitative.

Working Conditions and Health Risks

Factory work during the industrial era was characterized by long hours, poor working conditions, and significant health risks. Women, who were employed in industries such as textiles and garments, often worked up to 14 or 16 hours a day in cramped and poorly ventilated spaces (Foster & Clark, 2018). The repetitive nature of factory work, combined with inadequate safety measures, resulted in various health issues. Women faced respiratory problems from inhaling dust and fibers, physical injuries from operating machinery, and chronic fatigue from extended hours of labor (Cohen, n.d.).

The lack of safety regulations and the minimal attention given to workers' health further exacerbated these issues. For instance, factories often lacked proper fire exits or protections against dangerous machinery, increasing the risk of accidents and injuries (Cowan, 1976). The poor working conditions, coupled with insufficient pay, highlighted the exploitation of female labor in industrial settings, where women's work was undervalued compared to that of their male counterparts (Foster & Clark, 2018).

Child Labor and Family Dynamics

The industrial era also saw widespread use of child labor, which had additional implications for family dynamics. Economic necessity often led working-class families to rely on the wages earned by their children, who worked alongside their parents in factories under similarly harsh conditions (Stanfors & Goldscheider, 2017). This reliance on child labor not only disrupted children's education but also placed additional burdens on women, who had to manage both their own demanding work schedules and the well-being of their working children (Cohen, n.d.).

The integration of child labor into industrial workforces reflected broader social inequalities and reinforced gendered and age-based hierarchies within the workplace. Factory owners and managers exploited the vulnerability of women and children, paying them less and providing fewer protections compared to adult men (Foster & Clark, 2018). This exploitation exacerbated gender and age disparities, further complicating family dynamics as women struggled to balance their roles as workers and caregivers.

The Rise of Women in Urban Labor Markets

Despite the challenges posed by factory work, the industrial era also saw the emergence of new opportunities for women in urban labor markets. Women began to occupy various roles across different sectors, contributing significantly to both the economy and their families.

Types of Jobs and Economic Contributions

In urban settings, women found employment in a range of sectors beyond factory work, including domestic service, clerical work, teaching, and nursing. Each of these jobs came with its own set of challenges. Domestic service, for example, provided steady employment but often involved long hours, low wages, and limited personal freedom (Cohen, n.d.).

In contrast, clerical work, which expanded with the growth of administrative tasks in businesses and government, offered women more respectable and less physically demanding jobs. However, clerical positions were also characterized by strict gender-based wage disparities and limited opportunities for advancement (Foster & Clark, 2018).

Women's economic contributions were crucial, particularly in working-class families where their wages were essential for maintaining a basic standard of living. Women's participation in the workforce helped sustain urban economies and demonstrated their significant role in economic production (Stanfors & Goldscheider, 2017). Despite their contributions, women's work was often undervalued, reflecting broader gender inequalities within the labor market (Cowan, 1976).

The Growth of Female-Dominated Industries

The industrial era also saw the rise of female-dominated industries, such as textiles and garment production. These sectors employed large numbers of women because the work was seen as an extension of traditional "women's work" that required skills like nimble fingers and attention to detail (Foster & Clark, 2018). The prevalence of women in these industries often led to lower wages and poorer working conditions compared to male-dominated sectors, as employers justified these disparities by associating the work with traditional female roles (Cohen, n.d.).

Despite these challenges, female-dominated industries became important sites for labor organization and activism. Women workers began to form unions and participate in strikes to demand better wages, improved conditions, and fair treatment. This activism was crucial in advancing labor rights and highlighting gender-specific challenges within the workforce (Stanfors & Goldscheider, 2017).

The involvement of women in labor movements demonstrated their capacity for leadership and advocacy, challenging existing gender norms and contributing to the broader labor movement.

Early Labor Movements and Women's Participation

Women's involvement in early labor movements played a critical role in advocating for labor rights and improving working conditions. Their participation highlighted the importance of addressing gender-specific issues within the labor movement and contributed to broader efforts for social and economic change.

The Role of Women in Labor Unions

Women were instrumental in the formation and activities of early labor unions. Despite the male-dominated nature of many labor organizations, women workers took active roles in advocating for better working conditions and fair wages. For example, the Lowell Mill Girls, a group of female textile workers in Massachusetts, organized strikes in the 1830s and 1840s to protest wage cuts and harsh working conditions (Cohen, n.d.). These early labor actions were significant in demonstrating women's capacity to lead and organize within the labor movement.

Women's involvement in labor unions brought attention to gender-specific issues, such as sexual harassment and discrimination, and highlighted the need for greater protections and equity in the workplace (Foster & Clark, 2018). Their participation in labor movements underscored the importance of addressing these issues within the broader context of labor rights and social justice.

Key Strikes and Labor Actions Involving Women

Several significant strikes and labor actions involved women and highlighted their role in the labor movement. For instance, the 1909 "Uprising of the 20,000," a major strike by female garment workers in New York City, protested against poor working conditions and low wages in the garment industry (Stanfors & Goldscheider, 2017). This strike drew national attention to the struggles of women workers and led to some concessions from employers.

Similarly, the Lawrence Textile Strike of 1912, known as the "Bread and Roses Strike," saw women workers taking a leading role in demanding better pay and working conditions (Cohen, n.d.). The strike utilized innovative tactics, such as sending children to live with supporters in other cities, to gain public sympathy and support for their cause. These labor actions demonstrated the leadership and resilience of women workers and played a crucial role in advancing labor rights and highlighting gender-specific challenges within the workforce (Foster & Clark, 2018).

CHAPTER III

WOMEN'S ECONOMIC RIGHTS AND EMPOWERMENT ACROSS CONTEXTS

The struggle for women's economic rights has been a global movement, driven by the recognition that economic independence and equality are key to achieving true social empowerment. While specific movements have emerged in various regions, from Kerala to Mexico, and in historical contexts such as the women's liberation movement in the United States, these efforts share common themes of addressing wage inequality, improving education and employment opportunities, and challenging traditional gender roles.

Early Advocates and Their Economic Arguments

In Kerala, early feminist activists were primarily concerned with economic inequality, particularly wage disparities and the marginalization of women in the workforce. Despite Kerala's progress in education, activists pointed out that women remained economically disadvantaged compared to men, especially in insecure jobs like temporary or seasonal work, where they lacked benefits such as job security (Subrahmanian, 2019).

Similar economic arguments emerged in Mexico during the revolution, where women like Juana Belén Gutiérrez and Dolores Jiménez y Muro advocated for wage reforms. Jiménez's "Social and Political Plan" pushed for higher wages for both men and women, emphasizing that women's contributions to the workforce deserved recognition and equal treatment (Andrews, 2022). These early arguments highlight the central role that economic independence played in the broader movement for women's rights.

Economic Arguments for Women's Rights

The feminist movements across these contexts emphasized the critical nature of economic independence for women. In Kerala, feminist groups highlighted wage inequality and the lack of job security as major obstacles to women's empowerment. Activists also linked social issues like dowry and domestic violence to economic vulnerability, arguing that without financial independence, women remained trapped in patriarchal structures (Subrahmanian, 2019).

Similarly, during the women's liberation movement in the United States, feminists connected personal experiences of discrimination to broader economic inequalities, advocating for better economic opportunities and the dismantling of gender hierarchies. Women's suffrage in the late 19th and early 20th centuries led to significant shifts in legislative behavior in the U.S., resulting in increased public health spending and reforms that improved child welfare (Miller, 2008).

The Case for Women's Education and Employment

In all these movements, the importance of education and employment was recognized as vital for women's emancipation. In Kerala, despite high literacy rates, feminists argued that education alone was insufficient if it did not lead to meaningful employment opportunities that could offer economic security. Education had to be accompanied by job creation that allowed women to break out of the domestic sphere and achieve financial independence (Subrahmanian, 2019).

This echoed the broader global sentiment during the women's liberation movement, which also emphasized the need for women to access the workforce. Feminists in the United States challenged the assumption that education automatically led to equality, advocating for changes that would ensure women's participation in the labor market (Evans, 2015).

In Mexico, the revolution created unique opportunities for women to enter traditionally male-dominated fields like journalism, politics, and medicine. Activists like Hermila Galindo and Juana Belén Gutiérrez used their careers to demonstrate the importance of education and employment for women's independence, showcasing how access to professional opportunities could lead to broader economic empowerment (Andrews, 2022).

Economic Independence and Its Social Impact

Economic independence has consistently been seen as crucial for improving women's social status. In Kerala, the feminist movement highlighted how women's economic dependence on men reinforced their subjugation in the social hierarchy. By advocating for better wages and job security, the movement sought to dismantle traditional gender roles and empower women economically (Subrahmanian, 2019).

The suffrage movement in the United States had a similar impact, where the enfranchisement of women allowed them to influence public policies that aligned with their interests, particularly in the areas of child welfare and public health. The legislative changes that followed women's suffrage led to increased public health spending, which had broader social impacts, particularly in reducing child mortality and improving health infrastructure (Miller, 2008).

During the Mexican Revolution, women gained economic independence by stepping into roles that had previously been reserved for men. This period allowed women to redefine their social identities beyond the domestic sphere, increasing their autonomy and challenging traditional gender norms. High-ranking women such as María de la Luz Espinosa Barrera exemplified this shift, showing that women could lead and succeed in the military and other sectors traditionally dominated by men (Andrews, 2022).

Key Figures and Their Economic Impact

Across different contexts, key figures emerged who played significant roles in advancing women's economic rights. In Kerala, figures like Anna Chandy, India's first female judge, and K. Ajitha, a prominent activist, had a profound impact. Though Chandy did not explicitly identify as a feminist, her career broke barriers for women in politics and public life, indirectly contributing to their economic empowerment. Ajitha's activism, particularly her efforts to establish counseling centers for women, also contributed to the broader feminist agenda of economic justice (Subrahmanian, 2019).

In Mexico, women like Juana Belén Gutiérrez and Dolores Jiménez y Muro had significant economic and social impacts through their journalism and activism. Gutiérrez used her platform to highlight social injustices, while Jiménez's advocacy for workers' rights advanced the economic standing of women in Mexico (Andrews, 2022).

The Influence of Activists on Economic Policies

Activists in all these regions influenced economic policies by advocating for reforms that addressed gender disparities in the workplace. In Kerala, feminist interventions pushed for gender-sensitive approaches to wage inequality and domestic violence, creating pressure on policymakers to address these economic injustices (Subrahmanian, 2019). In the United States, activists within the women's suffrage movement successfully lobbied for public health spending that directly benefited women and children. This increased focus on hygiene and child welfare was a direct result of women's newfound political power, demonstrating their influence on economic policy (Miller, 2008).

In Mexico, activists like Dolores Jiménez y Muro played a direct role in influencing labor policies. Her writings on the need for wage reform and labor rights contributed to the introduction of reforms in the 1917 Constitution, such as paid maternity leave and childcare provisions, which had a lasting impact on working women in Mexico (Andrews, 2022).

The Role of Education in Economic Empowerment

Education was recognized as a key tool for economic empowerment across all contexts. In Kerala, feminists argued that without meaningful employment opportunities, education alone would not lead to economic empowerment for women (Subrahmanian, 2019). Similarly, in the U.S., the women's liberation movement emphasized the role of education in enabling women to participate fully in the workforce and achieve financial independence (Evans, 2015). In Mexico, women like Hermila Galindo used their positions in government and journalism to promote feminist ideals that linked education to broader social and economic reforms (Andrews, 2022).

Access to Education and Economic Opportunities

While access to education improved for women in many regions, this did not always translate into equal economic opportunities. In Kerala, despite high literacy rates, women continued to face difficulties in securing well-paying jobs, highlighting the need for reforms that would bridge the gap between education and economic independence (Subrahmanian, 2019). In the United States, women's access to education was crucial for breaking traditional gender roles and advocating for economic reforms that ensured equality in the workforce (Evans, 2015).

Educational Reforms and Their Economic Effects

Despite various educational reforms across these regions, the economic effects for women remained limited. In Kerala, feminists noted that even with high literacy rates, women continued to be marginalized in the workforce, calling for further reforms that would address systemic economic inequalities (Subrahmanian, 2019).

In the U.S., the women's liberation movement made it clear that broader access to education and professional training was necessary for women to achieve economic equality (Evans, 2015). Similarly, in Mexico, the advancements made by women in fields like journalism and politics during the revolution highlighted the need for further reforms to ensure women's access to both education and economic opportunities (Andrews, 2022).

Across various contexts, the fight for women's economic rights has been deeply connected to broader social and political movements. Whether in Kerala, Mexico, or the United States, the push for wage equality, access to education, and employment opportunities has been central to women's liberation. While significant progress has been made, the continued struggle for economic independence and equality remains a crucial aspect of the feminist movement globally.

CHAPTER IV

THE COMPREHENSIVE IMPACT OF WORLD WAR II ON WOMEN'S ECONOMIC ROLES

World War II marked a significant turning point for women's economic roles, reshaping their participation in the workforce, altering societal perceptions, and laying the foundation for future gender equality movements. As men left to fight in the war, the urgent need for labor in various sectors caused women to take on roles traditionally held by men. While the immediate post-war period saw a return to domesticity for many women, the long-term impact of their wartime contributions would be felt for decades, influencing labor laws, economic policies, and the broader feminist movement. This transformation can be examined in four phases: women's entry into the workforce during the war, economic shifts brought about by their participation, post-war transitions, and the long-term economic effects of their participation.

Women Entering the Workforce During WWII

The outbreak of World War II created an unprecedented labor shortage as millions of men were drafted into the armed forces. To fill the gap, the government and industries looked to women, encouraging them to take up jobs that had been traditionally reserved for men. Economic necessity was a primary driver of this shift, as many families relied on women's wages in the absence of male breadwinners. However, the rapid expansion of women in the workforce was not solely driven by necessity—it was also supported by a deliberate and extensive government propaganda campaign.

"Rosie the Riveter" became the most recognizable symbol of this movement. Rosie, depicted as a strong, capable woman working in factories, shipyards, and munitions plants, symbolized the essential role women were expected to play in the war effort. Government posters, films, and radio broadcasts celebrated women's participation, framing their labor as both a patriotic duty and a vital contribution to national security. These campaigns portrayed women not only as capable of performing jobs traditionally associated with men but also as proud contributors to the victory over the

Axis powers (Shatnawi & Fishback, 2018).

This shift in roles also reflected a profound change in societal attitudes toward women. Before the war, most women worked in domestic settings or in traditionally "feminine" jobs such as teaching, nursing, or secretarial work. However, with men fighting overseas, women entered industries like manufacturing, aviation, shipbuilding, and munitions production. They became welders, riveters, assembly line workers, and machinists, roles that required technical skill, strength, and stamina—jobs previously deemed unsuitable for women (Jaworski, 2014).

The percentage of women in the workforce rose dramatically during the war years, with 27.8% in 1940 climbing to 33.8% by 1945 (Goldin, 1991). Many of these women were not just young and single; they included married women and mothers, a demographic that had previously been discouraged from working outside the home. The war transformed the perception of women's capabilities, showing that they could balance both family and work responsibilities, even in demanding industrial roles.

The effect of this transition on women's clothing also highlights the broader cultural shift that was taking place. (Johnson, 2018) notes that during World War I, women's fashion had already begun to change to reflect their new roles in the workforce, with practical and functional garments replacing the elaborate and restrictive dresses of the pre-war period. Similarly, during World War II, women's clothing became more masculine and utilitarian, symbolizing their shift into jobs traditionally held by men. Trousers, jackets, and work uniforms became the standard attire for many women, reflecting their new responsibilities in the labor force.

Economic Shifts During WWII: Women in Wartime Industries

As the war progressed, women became an integral part of the wartime economy, particularly in industries directly related to military production. The shift was most visible in manufacturing sectors such as shipbuilding, aircraft production, and munitions. The rise of Rosie the Riveter reflected the strength, capability, and determination of women who took on roles traditionally filled by men. By 1943, women made up one-third of the workforce in war-related industries, contributing significantly to the production of planes, tanks, and weapons that were crucial to the war effort.

Women performed a wide range of tasks, from riveting metal in aircraft factories to operating heavy machinery in munitions plants. These roles required technical skills, physical endurance, and precision, breaking the traditional notion that women were suited only for domestic or "light" work. Rosie the Riveter not only motivated women to join the workforce but also helped change societal perceptions of women's abilities. For the first time, women were seen as essential workers in sectors critical to national security (Shatnawi & Fishback, 2018).

The increase in women's labor participation during the war had a profound economic impact. Women's wages, though still lower than those of men, improved during the war as the demand for labor surged. Many women experienced higher wages than they had before, giving them a new sense of economic independence. The war created a temporary breakdown of gender norms, allowing women to prove their value in roles that had previously been inaccessible.

However, the long-term effects of this shift were more complex. While women made significant contributions to the war economy, their employment was often viewed as temporary—a necessity during the war but not a permanent reconfiguration of the workforce. Despite their critical contributions, women were still paid less than men for doing the same work, and many faced the expectation that they would give up their jobs once the war ended and men returned home (Goldin, 1991).

Post-War Transitions and the Return to Traditional Roles

The end of World War II in 1945 brought significant challenges for women in the workforce. As soldiers returned from the front lines, they expected to reclaim their jobs, and women were pressured to return to their traditional roles as homemakers and mothers. The same propaganda machine that had encouraged women to work during the war now shifted to promoting domesticity, urging women to vacate their jobs and focus on family life (Shatnawi & Fishback, 2018).

Government policies and social pressures reinforced this return to traditional gender roles. Many industries laid off female workers to make room for returning male veterans, and the closure of wartime childcare facilities made it difficult for women with children to continue working. Women who wanted to remain in the workforce often faced discrimination and limited job opportunities. Employers were reluctant to hire women for high-paying industrial jobs, and many women were funneled back into lower-paying, traditionally female occupations such as clerical work, teaching, or nursing (Jaworski, 2014).

The decline in female labor force participation after the war was stark, but it was not total. Some women, particularly those who had gained new skills and a sense of economic independence, were determined to stay in the workforce. They faced significant challenges, including wage inequality, job insecurity, and societal expectations that they prioritize family over career. Despite these obstacles, the war had fundamentally altered the trajectory of women's participation in the labor market.

This post-war transition was also reflected in women's fashion. (Johnson, 2018) explains how World War I had initiated a trend toward more practical, masculine clothing for women, which was later replaced by more feminine attire as women returned to their domestic roles. Similarly, after World War II, the functional work uniforms that had become common during the war gave way to more traditional, decorative styles that emphasized femininity and domesticity. This shift in fashion symbolized the broader societal expectation that women should return to the home after their wartime service.

Long-Term Economic Effects of Wartime Participation

While the immediate post-war period saw a regression in women's employment, the experiences of women during World War II had lasting implications for their economic roles and rights. The war had demonstrated that women were not only capable of performing jobs in traditionally male-dominated industries but were also essential to the success of the national economy. This realization laid the foundation for future movements advocating gender equality in the workplace (Goldin, 1991).

The war highlighted the need for changes in labor laws and policies. Although progress was slow, women's wartime participation raised awareness about issues such as wage inequality, discrimination in hiring, and the lack of childcare facilities for working mothers. These issues would become central to the feminist movements of the 1960s and 1970s, which sought to address the systemic barriers that women faced in the labor market (Shatnawi & Fishback, 2018).

The war also inspired a cultural shift in the way women viewed their roles in society. Women who had gained economic independence and personal fulfillment through their work were less willing to accept the limited opportunities available to them after the war. Their experiences during WWII encouraged future generations to challenge traditional gender roles and demand greater access to education, employment, and leadership positions.

(Johnson, 2018) notes a similar long-term impact of World War I on women's roles. The shift towards practical, functional clothing during the war symbolized women's growing independence and participation in the public sphere. This trend continued into the flapper era of the 1920s, which represented a rejection of traditional gender roles and a desire for greater personal freedom. The experiences of women during World War II had a comparable impact, setting the stage for future movements that would challenge the societal expectations that confined women to domestic roles and limited their opportunities for economic advancement.

World War II was a transformative period for women's economic roles, reshaping the labor market and challenging traditional gender norms. Women's participation in the workforce during the war not only filled a critical labor shortage but also proved their capabilities in industries and jobs that had previously been inaccessible to them. While the post-war period brought significant challenges as women were pressured to return to their domestic roles, the long-term effects of their wartime participation would influence future movements for gender equality and labor rights.

The experiences of women during World War II, along with the cultural and economic shifts that accompanied their participation in the workforce, laid the groundwork for future changes in labor policies and societal attitudes toward women's work. This period marked the beginning of a gradual but significant shift toward greater recognition of women's contributions to the economy, inspiring future generations to fight for equal rights and opportunities in the workforce. The legacy of World War II on women's economic roles continues to influence modern debates about gender equality and the ongoing pursuit of economic justice.

CHAPTER V

THE POST-WAR BOOM AND THE FEMINIST MOVEMENT

Economic Growth and Increased Opportunities for Women

The post-World War II era marked a period of significant transformation for women's roles in the workforce and society at large. Before and during the war, women had been encouraged to take on roles traditionally held by men, particularly in industries and public services. As men went off to fight, women filled the vacancies left behind, experiencing unprecedented economic independence. However, after the war ended, many societies attempted to revert to pre-war gender norms, with the expectation that women would return to domestic roles.

Despite these societal pressures, the economic necessity and the momentum gained from their wartime contributions allowed women to continue advancing in the workforce. This period saw a significant rise in women's economic participation, leading to their involvement in movements for social change, such as the feminist antimilitarist movement. According to (Cashdan, 1989), women began to use their economic power not only to sustain their households but also to advocate for peace and social justice. This shift was particularly visible in their participation in anti-nuclear protests, where they emphasized decentralization and direct participation in political activism. Unlike previous eras, women were not merely supporting male-led movements but were central to the leadership, reshaping the objectives and strategies of the causes they championed (Cashdan, 1989).

The expansion of economic opportunities for women is also analyzed through different theoretical lenses. World Culture Theory (WCT) posits that societal changes, including the broadening of economic roles for women, are the result of the diffusion of global norms and values. These norms, often propagated by international bodies like NGOs and multinational institutions, promote gender equality, which gradually permeates local cultures and policies. As these global norms spread, they influence local legislation regarding women's education, labor participation, and access to resources, ultimately leading to expanded economic opportunities for women (Stromquist, 2015).

On the other hand, World System Analysis (WSA) offers a more critical interpretation, rooted in political struggle and the dynamics of global capitalism. According to WSA, the increased economic opportunities for women, particularly in developing nations, are not simply a reflection of global cultural diffusion but a result of ongoing conflicts between marginalized groups (including women) and dominant capitalist systems. Women's labor force participation is often driven by the demands of the global capitalist economy, which relies heavily on cheap labor, particularly from women in peripheral nations. In this context, the feminization of labor—where women take on low-wage, precarious jobs—reflects broader patterns of global economic inequality, rather than a straightforward empowerment of women (Stromquist, 2015).

The Second Wave of Feminism and Its Economic Agenda

The Second Wave of feminism, which emerged in the 1960s and 1970s, represented a radical shift in how women viewed their roles in both society and the economy. This wave of feminism was closely tied to larger social and political movements, such as anti-imperialist and anti-war efforts, with feminists recognizing the deep connections between sexism, war, and economic exploitation. Feminists in this era understood that the fight for women's rights could not be separated from broader economic and social struggles. As (Cashdan, 1989) notes, the feminist movement began to emphasize decentralization and the importance of linking women's rights with global solidarity, particularly with women in the developing world who faced compounded oppression due to both gender and economic exploitation.

The economic agenda of the Second Wave of feminism was focused on addressing systemic inequalities that kept women economically disadvantaged. Feminists pushed for equal pay, reproductive rights, and better labor conditions, arguing that these were not just "women's issues" but fundamental rights that were deeply connected to the structure of the global capitalist economy (Vellacott, 1987). These demands were particularly relevant for working-class women, whose economic exploitation was often exacerbated by their roles as primary caregivers within the household. The feminist movement during this period increasingly aligned itself with socialist ideologies, arguing that capitalism and militarism were inherently patriarchal systems that needed to be dismantled in order to achieve true gender equality (Vellacott, 1987).

World Culture Theory (WCT) frames this feminist agenda as part of a broader cultural shift toward human rights and individual empowerment. According to WCT, the spread of feminist ideas during the 1960s and 1970s was driven by the global diffusion of human rights discourse, which gained momentum after World War II. International organizations such as the United Nations played a critical role in promoting gender equality as a universal value, leading to the adoption of policies that advanced women's rights across the globe (Stromquist, 2015).

In contrast, World System Analysis (WSA) views the gains made by feminists in this period as the result of anti-systemic movements that sought to challenge the structures of global capitalism. WSA argues that women's demands for economic equality, reproductive rights, and better labor conditions were not simply the result of a cultural shift but were part of broader struggles against capitalist exploitation. Feminists were not just seeking inclusion within the existing system but were advocating for systemic change that addressed the root causes of economic and gender inequality (Stromquist, 2015).

Changing Family Dynamics and Labor Force Participation

The rise of the feminist movement also brought about significant changes in family dynamics. As more women entered the workforce, the traditional family model, where the man was the breadwinner and the woman was the homemaker, began to break down. Dual-income households became more common, with women contributing to the family's economic stability while also balancing domestic responsibilities. This shift in family dynamics reflected broader societal changes in gender roles and expectations, as women began to challenge the notion that their primary responsibility was to the home and family (Vellacott, 1987).

However, the increasing participation of women in the labor force also highlighted the persistent challenges women faced in balancing work and family life. Even as women took on more economic responsibilities, they were still expected to manage the majority of domestic duties, leading to what feminists called the "double burden." This struggle was not just an individual issue but a reflection of broader societal expectations and the failure of social support systems to adapt to the changing realities of women's lives (Walker, 1985).

World Culture Theory (WCT) explains these shifts as part of the global diffusion of norms that promote gender equality and modern family life. The spread of feminist ideas, particularly those related to women's rights in the workplace and the family, contributed to the redefinition of traditional family structures. According to WCT, as these global norms spread, they influenced local policies and practices, leading to more women entering the workforce and balancing professional and family responsibilities (Stromquist, 2015).

In contrast, World System Analysis (WSA) provides a more critical perspective, arguing that the rise of dual-income households was driven by economic necessity within the capitalist world system. According to WSA, the increasing need for two incomes in many households was not simply a reflection of changing cultural norms but a response to economic pressures created by global capitalism. In many cases, women entered the workforce in low-paying, precarious jobs, which were an extension of their traditional domestic roles, such as caregiving and teaching. This division of labor reinforced existing gender inequalities and made it difficult for women to achieve true economic independence (Stromquist, 2015).

Women in Higher Education and Professional Fields

The post-war period also saw significant progress in women's access to higher education and professional fields. As more women enrolled in universities, they began to break into fields that had traditionally been dominated by men, such as law, medicine, and academia. This expansion into higher education was critical for the feminist movement, as educated women brought new philosophical perspectives to feminist theory and activism. These women were often at the forefront of movements advocating for decentralized leadership and more inclusive organizational structures, challenging traditional hierarchies within both academia and activism (Cashdan, 1989).

World Culture Theory (WCT) views the increasing presence of women in higher education as a success of modern rational thought and the diffusion of global norms that promote gender equality. According to WCT, as these norms spread, they led to increased access to education for women, allowing them to enter fields traditionally dominated by men (Stromquist, 2015). However, WCT tends to focus on the symbolic progress of educational expansion without fully addressing the persistent challenges women face in these fields, such as gender segregation and the undervaluation of women's labor.

World System Analysis (WSA) provides a more critical lens, arguing that while more women are entering higher education and professional fields, they continue to face significant structural barriers. WSA points out that women are often concentrated in lower-paying professions, such as education and social sciences, while men dominate higher-paying fields like engineering and technology. This gender segregation is not merely a reflection of cultural norms but is tied to the global capitalist system, which values certain types of labor over others. WSA emphasizes that even as women enter professional fields, they continue to face wage gaps, limited access to leadership positions, and the burden of unpaid domestic labor (Stromquist, 2015).

Integration of Feminism, Pacifism, and Socialism

Marshall and Helena Swanwick believed that militarism and capitalism were inherently oppressive to women and that true equality could only be achieved by dismantling the structures that perpetuated war and economic exploitation (Vellacott, 1987). These women argued that a militaristic society was not just harmful to men, who were sent off to fight, but also to women, who were left to pick up the pieces and manage the domestic front during times of war.

The Women's International League for Peace and Freedom (WILPF), founded in 1915, was a significant achievement of the feminist pacifist movement. WILPF provided a platform for women to voice their opposition to war and advocate for a new world order based on cooperation, peace, and gender equality. The feminist pacifists believed that women's nurturing qualities made them uniquely suited to lead in matters of peace and conflict resolution, and they sought to reimagine a world in which women played a central role in decision-making (Vellacott, 1987).

This integration of feminism, pacifism, and socialism represented a radical departure from traditional feminist goals, which had often focused on achieving equality within the existing male-dominated system. Instead, these women envisioned a new political order that was inherently less violent and more inclusive, with women at the forefront of efforts to create a just and peaceful society (Vellacott, 1987).

The post-war feminist movements and the Second Wave of feminism illustrate the complex interplay between economic growth, cultural diffusion, and political struggle in shaping women's roles. World Culture Theory emphasizes the role of global institutions and norms in promoting gender equality, while World System Analysis highlights the economic and political struggles women have faced in their fight for true equality. Both perspectives offer valuable insights into the global expansion of feminist ideas, revealing the ongoing challenges women encounter as they strive for economic independence, social justice, and political power.

CHAPTER VI

THE GLOBAL SOUTH AND WOMEN'S ECONOMIC DEVELOPMENT

The economic empowerment of women in the Global South represents a crucial yet complex issue, deeply intertwined with the broader development trajectory of the region. Women's roles in agriculture, the informal sector, and small-scale entrepreneurship are pivotal to household survival, community well-being, and overall economic stability. Yet, systemic barriers, rooted in gender inequality, persistently hinder their full economic participation. Understanding the depth and breadth of these challenges requires an exploration of women's contributions to these sectors, the unique obstacles they face in rural versus urban environments, and the impact of education and microfinance. Additionally, the role of non-governmental organizations (NGOs) and international aid is instrumental in driving progress, though long-term success hinges on empowering women to be active agents in shaping their own futures.

Women's Contributions to Agriculture and the Informal Sector

Women in the Global South form the backbone of agricultural production and the informal economy. In many developing countries, they are responsible for a significant portion of small-scale farming, often producing food for both household consumption and local markets. Their contributions extend beyond merely sustaining their families; they play a critical role in ensuring food security at the community level. Women cultivate crops, manage livestock, and engage in post-harvest activities, all while balancing domestic responsibilities. Their efforts are essential for economic resilience, particularly in rural areas where agriculture is the main source of livelihood (Duflo, 2012).

Despite this, women's contributions to agriculture are frequently overlooked. They face limited access to key resources, such as land ownership, which is often controlled by male family members or subject to discriminatory inheritance laws. Without secure land tenure, women are restricted in their ability to make long-term investments in agricultural productivity. Additionally, access to credit and agricultural inputs, such as fertilizers and tools, remains inadequate for many women, further constraining their productivity and economic potential. These barriers perpetuate a cycle of poverty and economic dependence, where women are unable to fully benefit from the value they generate through their labor.

In parallel, the informal sector serves as a crucial economic outlet for women, particularly in urban areas. Here, women engage in street vending, home-based businesses, and small-scale trading, utilizing the flexibility of informal work to balance income generation with caregiving responsibilities. The informal economy offers women the opportunity to exercise entrepreneurial ingenuity, yet it remains fraught with challenges. Informal work is often precarious, lacking legal protections, job security, or benefits such as healthcare and pensions. Moreover, the work is undervalued and unregulated, leaving women vulnerable to exploitation and harassment. In Haiti, for instance, women are central to both agriculture and informal economic activities, yet their labor is often seen as an extension of their traditional domestic roles, limiting their prospects for financial independence and economic mobility (Mauconduit et al., 2013).

Challenges Faced by Women in Rural and Urban Settings

The challenges women face in their economic endeavors are shaped by the geographical, social, and economic contexts in which they live. Rural and urban environments present distinct barriers, though both contexts are underpinned by systemic gender inequalities that limit women's access to resources, education, and formal employment opportunities.

In rural areas, traditional gender roles are often deeply entrenched. Women are expected to manage household responsibilities while contributing to agricultural work, a dual burden that leaves little room for personal or economic advancement. Social norms often restrict women's mobility, limiting their access to markets, training, or employment opportunities outside their immediate communities. Furthermore, rural women typically have less access to healthcare and education, services that are crucial for improving productivity and well-being. For instance, in many rural regions, women work alongside men in agriculture, yet they are far less likely to own land or control the income derived from their labor. This lack of control over assets reinforces their dependence on male family members and perpetuates cycles of poverty and economic insecurity (Islam, 2011).

Urban settings, while offering more opportunities for formal education and employment, are not without their challenges. Women in urban areas often find themselves trapped in low-paying, insecure jobs that provide little in the way of career advancement or financial stability. Discrimination in the labor market remains a pervasive issue, with women frequently facing wage gaps and barriers to promotions in comparison to their male counterparts. The burden of unpaid domestic work, such as childcare and eldercare, also remains heavy in urban areas, as women juggle these responsibilities alongside formal employment. This "double burden" of paid and unpaid work limits the time and energy women can devote to advancing their careers or improving their economic standing (Duflo, 2012).

The social norms that dictate gender roles in both rural and urban settings are significant obstacles to women's economic empowerment. In many cases, these norms are upheld by legal frameworks that limit women's rights to property, inheritance, and employment. Changing these norms requires not only legal reform but also community-level interventions that challenge the deep-rooted cultural beliefs that sustain gender inequality.

Microfinance and Women's Entrepreneurship

Microfinance has emerged as one of the most influential tools for promoting women's economic empowerment in the Global South, particularly through entrepreneurship. The availability of small loans to women, often with few or no collateral requirements, has provided millions with the financial capital needed to start or expand small businesses. These businesses, ranging from agricultural ventures to retail and service enterprises, allow women to generate income, support their families, and contribute to local economies. In Bangladesh and India, for example, microfinance initiatives have been instrumental in helping women lift themselves and their families out of poverty, fostering both financial independence and social empowerment (Islam, 2011).

However, microfinance is not without its challenges and limitations. Access to credit alone does not guarantee business success. Many women, particularly those in rural areas, face difficulties in accessing markets and lack the financial literacy or business skills necessary to grow their enterprises. Without adequate training and support, some women find themselves struggling to repay loans, particularly when faced with high-interest rates and fluctuating market conditions. This can lead to a phenomenon known as "empowerment debt," where the financial pressures of loan repayment outweigh the benefits of the initial credit. In such cases, microfinance can exacerbate economic vulnerabilities rather than alleviate them (Ojediran & Anderson, 2020).

The success of microfinance initiatives depends heavily on the provision of complementary services, such as business training, mentoring, and access to markets. Women need the tools to manage their finances, understand market trends, and grow their businesses sustainably. Additionally, the socio-cultural context in which microfinance operates is critical. In patriarchal societies, women's control over financial resources can be challenged by male family members, limiting the potential for true financial independence. Addressing these broader structural barriers is essential for microfinance to fulfill its promise as a tool for women's empowerment.

Education and Its Impact on Women's Economic Status

Education is widely recognized as a key determinant of women's economic empowerment. Educated women are more likely to participate in the formal labor market, earn higher incomes, and make informed decisions that affect their families and communities. Vocational training and literacy programs, particularly those tailored to women's specific needs and circumstances, can significantly enhance their employability and economic potential. Basic literacy enables women to engage in more complex financial transactions, understand their rights, and access new opportunities in both formal and informal economies (Duflo, 2012).

In many parts of the Global South, however, education remains a significant barrier to women's empowerment, particularly in rural areas. Girls are often kept out of school due to traditional gender roles that prioritize domestic duties over formal education. Even when girls do attend school, they often face challenges such as poor-quality education, early marriage, and a lack of female role models in professional fields. Furthermore, education systems in many countries are underfunded and ill-equipped to address the specific needs of girls, particularly in rural regions where access to schools is limited. This gap in education limits women's ability to secure well-paying jobs, further entrenching cycles of poverty and dependence (Licumba et al., 2016).

Investment in girls' education has been shown to yield substantial returns, both for individuals and for broader economic development. Educated women are more likely to delay marriage and childbirth, invest in their children's education, and contribute to higher household incomes. Studies have consistently demonstrated that improving access to education, particularly at the secondary and tertiary levels, is one of the most effective strategies for promoting gender equality and driving economic growth.

Role of NGOs and International Aid in Supporting Women's Empowerment

Non-governmental organizations (NGOs) and international aid agencies play a crucial role in supporting the economic empowerment of women in the Global South. These organizations often serve as intermediaries, providing women with access to financial resources, technical expertise, and training that would otherwise be unavailable to them. Programs designed by NGOs, such as the Women's Opportunity Project in Rwanda, have demonstrated the powerful ripple effects that targeted interventions can have on women's economic empowerment, local economies, and community well-being (Duflo, 2012).

However, the effectiveness of these programs depends on their ability to engage women as active participants in their own development. Too often, international aid efforts adopt a top-down approach, where external organizations design and implement programs without fully understanding the local context or involving women in decision-making processes. This can lead to programs that are not sustainable or do not address the root causes of gender inequality. Instead, sustainable development models must focus on building local capacity and ensuring that women have a voice in shaping the programs that affect their lives (Islam, 2011).

Long-term success in promoting women's economic empowerment requires a holistic approach that addresses not only economic barriers but also the social and cultural norms that underpin gender inequality. International aid can play a crucial role in driving this change, but it must be delivered in a way that empowers women to be active agents in their own futures.

The economic empowerment of women in the Global South is both a driver of development and an outcome of broader social and economic progress. Women play indispensable roles in agriculture and the informal sector, yet their contributions are often undervalued due to systemic barriers rooted in gender inequality. Addressing these barriers requires a multifaceted approach that includes improving access to education, healthcare, credit, and markets, while simultaneously challenging discriminatory social norms and policies. Empowering women economically not only benefits individual families but also generates positive ripple effects that contribute to the development and well-being of entire communities

CHAPTER VII

WOMEN IN LEADERSHIP AND CORPORATE POWER

The journey of women into leadership has been long, marked by both challenges and triumphs. Historically, women have been significantly underrepresented in corporate leadership positions, particularly in the executive roles of Fortune 500 companies. This disparity is not only evident in the number of women CEOs but also in boardrooms and financial leadership positions (Zhang & Yu, 2020). The so-called "glass ceiling" has proven to be a persistent barrier for women, an invisible but powerful obstacle that has kept them from advancing to the highest echelons of leadership. This metaphorical ceiling is reinforced by a variety of factors, including both organizational biases and societal expectations.

One of the central issues contributing to this phenomenon is the perception that women often lack critical experience in line management roles—positions that traditionally lead to executive leadership. Moreover, gender stereotypes that paint women as too emotional, collaborative, or risk-averse also play a significant role in their exclusion from leadership opportunities (Zhang & Yu, 2020). The structural nature of these biases is also compounded by male-dominated recruitment networks and informal hiring practices that further perpetuate gender inequality in leadership (Testy, 2019).

Breaking the Glass Ceiling

While the barriers are formidable, many women leaders are actively challenging and shattering the glass ceiling. A major strategy they employ is consistently exceeding performance expectations to counteract gendered misconceptions about their capabilities (Zhang & Yu, 2020). Women are also increasingly adopting a collaborative work style and actively seeking high-visibility assignments to ensure their contributions are noticed and valued. In these male-dominated spaces, visibility and exceptional performance have become critical tools for overcoming entrenched biases.

In addition, mentorship and networking are invaluable resources for women navigating leadership challenges. Many have found that mentors provide crucial guidance and access to opportunities, helping them advance despite the barriers in place. Moreover, as women gain more international experience and pursue advanced educational credentials, they further bolster their qualifications, making it harder for organizations to deny them positions of influence (Trinh et al., 2018). These strategies demonstrate how women are using individual agency to rise within the corporate ranks, while also highlighting the importance of organizational support in this process.

The Business Case for Gender Diversity

Beyond the personal success stories, the inclusion of women in leadership has broader implications for corporate success. Research has repeatedly demonstrated that gender-diverse leadership teams outperform their male-dominated counterparts. Companies with more women on their boards tend to exhibit better financial performance and stronger governance (Gonçalves et al., 2022). This correlation between gender diversity and profitability makes a compelling case for businesses to actively dismantle the barriers that prevent women from advancing.

In fact, companies that embrace gender diversity benefit from improved decision-making and greater innovation. Women bring unique perspectives and leadership styles to the table, fostering environments that are more collaborative and inclusive. This diversity of thought is crucial in today's complex business landscape, where flexibility and adaptability are key to navigating the challenges of a globalized economy (Pierli et al., 2022). Moreover, gender-diverse teams are more likely to understand and meet the needs of diverse customer bases, further enhancing business success.

Women's Leadership in Sustainability

One particularly striking area where women leaders are making a significant impact is in the realm of corporate sustainability. Women often bring a more holistic approach to leadership, considering not only the financial bottom line but also the social and environmental implications of their decisions (Pierli et al., 2022). This ability to see the interconnectedness of economic, social, and environmental factors makes women particularly adept at steering organizations toward sustainable business practices. Female leaders tend to prioritize long-term gains over short-term profits, pushing for strategies that ensure environmental conservation and social responsibility.

For example, women leaders have been found to champion initiatives that focus on responsible waste management, resource conservation, and the promotion of local employment opportunities. By fostering a culture of sustainability, these leaders are not only helping their organizations reduce their environmental footprint but are also contributing to the broader goal of sustainable development. However, the challenges they face in this regard are significant. Gender biases and a lack of support from senior management often hinder their efforts to promote sustainability effectively (Pierli et al., 2022).

The Impact of Female Leadership on Corporate Performance

Research has shown that the presence of women in leadership positions can have a significant positive impact on firm performance. Companies with female leaders tend to exhibit stronger financial health, improved governance, and better risk management practices (Gonçalves et al., 2022). In particular, having women in boardrooms is linked to more balanced decision-making and enhanced board monitoring. However, this is not a straightforward relationship. While the presence of female Chairpersons has been positively associated with firm value, the presence of female CEOs has shown mixed results, with some studies suggesting that they face greater scrutiny and higher expectations compared to their male counterparts (Trinh et al., 2018).

The mixed findings underscore the complexities of gender dynamics in leadership. While women bring valuable perspectives and strengths to the table, the environment in which they lead can sometimes amplify the challenges they face. For example, gender differences in communication styles and risk aversion may influence how their leadership is perceived and its subsequent impact on corporate performance (Gonçalves et al., 2022). Nevertheless, the overall trend indicates that gender diversity in leadership is a net positive for organizations, particularly when supported by inclusive corporate cultures.

Overcoming Challenges and Moving Forward

Despite the progress that has been made, women in leadership continue to face significant challenges. Unconscious biases remain deeply ingrained in corporate cultures, often manifesting in subtle but impactful ways. These biases can influence hiring and promotion decisions, making it harder for women to break through to top leadership positions (Zhang & Yu, 2020). Additionally, the work-life balance remains a concern, as many women still shoulder the majority of caregiving responsibilities, making the demands of executive roles even more challenging (Testy, 2019).

To address these challenges, organizations need to take a proactive approach. This includes implementing training programs aimed at mitigating unconscious biases, offering mentorship and leadership development opportunities tailored to women, and creating flexible work arrangements that accommodate the demands of both professional and personal life (Pierli et al., 2022). Moreover, expanding the talent pipeline by broadening the criteria for leadership positions and actively recruiting women from diverse backgrounds can help accelerate the pace of gender equality in leadership.

In the end, breaking the glass ceiling is not just about individual effort. It requires a concerted effort from both organizations and society to dismantle the structural barriers that have long held women back. The journey is far from over, but with continued advocacy and intentional action, the future of women in leadership looks increasingly promising. By embracing the unique strengths women bring to leadership, businesses and economies stand to benefit immensely from their contributions. As the evidence continues to mount, it becomes ever clearer that gender diversity in leadership is not just a matter of fairness—it is a smart business strategy.

CHAPTER VIII

THE GENDER PAY GAP AND ECONOMIC DISPARITIES

The gender wealth gap is one of the most persistent forms of economic inequality, deeply intertwined with societal norms, structural barriers, and historical legacies of discrimination. This gap refers to the significant disparity in the accumulation of assets and net worth between men and women, often resulting in women's financial insecurity, especially as they age. Unlike the gender pay gap, which focuses on the income earned by men and women during their working lives, the wealth gap captures the long-term consequences of unequal income distribution, unpaid labor, and financial decision-making opportunities. The accumulation of wealth over a lifetime is influenced by several factors, including income, family responsibilities, career interruptions, investment behavior, and societal norms around gender roles. These disparities are particularly stark in countries with a wide gender pay gap, such as Estonia, which holds the dubious distinction of having the largest gender wage gap in the European Union (Meriküll et al., 2021).

In many societies, traditional gender roles still dictate the allocation of responsibilities within households, with women taking on a disproportionate share of caregiving duties and unpaid labor. This dynamic inevitably interrupts women's career progression, reducing their opportunities for wealth accumulation. The research suggests that wealth accumulation mirrors income patterns, meaning that persistent income inequality over the years leads to a gender wealth gap that widens over time. This gap is not merely an economic anomaly but a reflection of how societal values around gender roles influence financial outcomes. In most cases, women's economic independence is hampered by the same societal expectations that push them into unpaid caregiving and low-paying professions, reinforcing the economic disparity between the sexes.

Career interruptions due to childbirth and childcare responsibilities are significant contributors to the gender pay and wealth gap. Women's earnings often stagnate or decline during these periods, while men's careers typically continue uninterrupted, allowing them to accumulate more wealth. These career breaks affect women's ability to contribute to retirement savings, pensions, and other financial investments, further exacerbating the wealth gap. The decision to work part-time, frequently made by women to balance family responsibilities, also plays a critical role in this economic disparity (Litman et al., 2020). Part-time work typically offers lower wages, fewer benefits, and limited opportunities for career advancement, which not only affects women's earnings in the present but also reduces their long-term financial security. Occupational segregation, where women are concentrated in lower-paying, female-dominated industries, compounds the problem. While men dominate higher-paying sectors like technology and engineering, women are overrepresented in caregiving, education, and administrative roles, which are undervalued and underpaid (Meriküll et al., 2021).

Long-Term Economic Consequences for Women and Families: Perpetuating Cycles of Poverty

The economic consequences of the gender wealth gap extend far beyond the individual women affected. When women earn less and accumulate less wealth, their families and future generations are also disadvantaged. Lower lifetime earnings limit women's ability to save, invest, and build financial security, making them more vulnerable to economic shocks and financial insecurity in retirement. This financial precariousness is passed down to their children, who may have fewer resources for education, healthcare, and overall well-being. The gender wealth gap, therefore, perpetuates cycles of poverty that can span generations (Nguyen et al., 2020). Women's reduced financial capacity also means that they have less to pass on to their children in terms of intergenerational wealth, further widening the wealth gap between men and women.

The impact on children is particularly profound. When women have fewer financial resources, they are often unable to invest in their children's education or other developmental opportunities, which can affect their children's future earning potential. This perpetuates a cycle of disadvantage, as the children of women who face economic hardship are more likely to experience economic challenges themselves. The research highlights how these financial limitations not only affect individual households but also have broader societal implications, as economic inequalities are passed down from one generation to the next (Nguyen et al., 2020). This transmission of economic disadvantage across generations underscores the importance of addressing the structural barriers that contribute to the gender wealth gap. It is not just a matter of individual women earning less or saving less; it is a systemic issue that affects families, communities, and entire societies.

The Impact of Retirement Savings and Financial Security: Women's Vulnerability in Old Age

Retirement savings are one of the most critical areas where the gender wealth gap manifests, often with devastating consequences for women as they age. Women typically live longer than men, which means they need more savings to support themselves throughout retirement. However, due to the gender pay gap and career interruptions, women accumulate significantly less in retirement savings, pensions, and other long-term financial investments. This leaves many women financially vulnerable in their later years, with a higher risk of poverty and dependence on social welfare programs (Kim et al., 2023). The disparity in retirement savings is a direct result of the cumulative effects of earning less over a lifetime, having less disposable income to save, and often prioritizing family financial needs over personal retirement planning.

The issue of retirement insecurity is particularly concerning for single women and widows, who may not have the financial support of a spouse's income or savings. Women who have spent much of their lives caring for family members or working in part-time, low-wage jobs may find themselves with little to no savings as they enter retirement. This financial precariousness forces many women to rely on public assistance or continue working well into old age, even when their health and circumstances make it difficult to do so. The research underscores the importance of addressing the structural barriers that prevent women from building adequate retirement savings, including the need for policies that promote equal pay, better access to retirement plans, and financial education that empowers women to take control of their financial futures (Kim et al., 2023).

The broader societal implications of this retirement insecurity are significant. As more women enter retirement without sufficient savings, the burden on social welfare systems increases, straining public resources and exacerbating economic inequality. The lack of financial independence among older women also limits their ability to contribute to their communities and families, further perpetuating cycles of economic disadvantage. Addressing the gender wealth gap in retirement savings is not just about ensuring individual financial security; it is about promoting economic stability and equity on a societal level.

Occupational Segregation: How Gendered Labor Markets Reinforce Inequality

Occupational segregation is one of the most entrenched forms of gender inequality in the labor market and plays a critical role in the gender wealth gap. Women are disproportionately concentrated in lower-paying, female-dominated industries, while men are overrepresented in higher-paying fields such as technology, engineering, and finance. This division of labor is not only a reflection of personal preferences or career choices but is heavily influenced by societal norms, expectations, and structural barriers that steer men and women into different career paths. Women's work is often undervalued, both in terms of wages and societal recognition, which contributes to the persistent wage and wealth gap (Meriküll et al., 2021).

The caregiving sector, for example, is overwhelmingly dominated by women, yet it is one of the lowest-paying industries despite its critical role in society. Professions such as nursing, teaching, and social work, which are essential to the well-being of communities, are typically underpaid compared to male-dominated professions that require similar levels of education and expertise. This undervaluation of "women's work" reinforces the gender wealth gap, as women in these professions have fewer opportunities to accumulate wealth over their lifetimes. The research highlights how societal expectations around gender roles contribute to this occupational segregation, as women are often expected to take on caregiving responsibilities both at home and in their careers, limiting their access to higher-paying industries (Meriküll et al., 2021).

Moreover, even within the same professions, women tend to be concentrated in lower-paying positions or are less likely to advance to leadership roles compared to their male counterparts. This is particularly evident in fields like academia, where women are underrepresented in senior faculty positions and are more likely to be in lower-paying, teaching-focused roles rather than research-intensive or administrative positions. The research in this area suggests that institutional biases, such as gender discrimination in hiring and promotion, contribute to this unequal distribution of opportunities (Litman et al., 2020). These disparities within professions further reinforce the gender wealth gap, as women are systematically denied the opportunities for career advancement and wealth accumulation that are available to men.

The Gender Pay Gap in Online Labor Markets: The Persistence of Inequality

In recent years, the rise of online labor markets, such as Amazon Mechanical Turk (MTurk), has been touted as a potential equalizer for workers, offering flexible opportunities for people to earn money regardless of their location, background, or personal circumstances. However, even in these seemingly neutral environments, the gender pay gap persists. The research highlights how women on MTurk tend to select lower-paying tasks compared to men, despite having similar qualifications and experience (Litman et al., 2020). This behavior may be influenced by broader societal norms around gender and work, as well as women's lower reservation wages or differing expectations regarding compensation.

The persistence of the gender pay gap in online labor markets challenges the notion that flexible, gig-based work can serve as a solution to traditional labor market inequalities. While online platforms like MTurk offer greater flexibility for workers, particularly women who may need to balance paid work with caregiving responsibilities, they do not eliminate the structural barriers that contribute to wage inequality. Women on these platforms are still subject to the same societal pressures and expectations that shape their work behavior in traditional labor markets, such as the tendency to undervalue their labor and prioritize lower-paying, flexible work over higher-paying opportunities.

The research also points out that online labor platforms have the potential to address these disparities by implementing mechanisms such as gender quotas in task selection or offering transparent pay information to ensure equal pay for equal work (Litman et al., 2020). However, without systemic changes in how society values women's work and addresses the structural barriers that limit their economic opportunities, the gender pay gap will continue to persist in both traditional and online labor markets.

Policy Interventions and Corporate Practices: The Path to Gender Equity

Addressing the gender wealth and pay gap requires comprehensive policy interventions and corporate practices that tackle the root causes of economic inequality. Pay transparency, anti-discrimination laws, and policies promoting equal pay for equal work are critical to closing the gap (Nguyen et al., 2020). Legislation that mandates pay transparency can help identify and address wage disparities within organizations, ensuring that women are paid fairly for their work. Anti-discrimination laws, particularly those that protect against gender bias in hiring, promotion, and compensation, are also essential for creating a more equitable labor market.

Corporate practices, such as offering flexible work arrangements, family-friendly policies, and unconscious bias training, are equally important in promoting gender equity in the workplace. Many women face significant barriers to advancing in their careers due to the lack of flexible work options that accommodate caregiving responsibilities. Companies that offer flexible schedules, remote work opportunities, and paid family leave can help mitigate the impact of career interruptions on women's earnings and long-term financial security. Unconscious bias training can also help address the implicit stereotypes and assumptions that often influence hiring, promotion, and pay decisions, ensuring that women have equal opportunities for career advancement (Nguyen et al., 2020).

While these policy interventions and corporate practices are critical steps toward closing the gender wealth and pay gap, they are not a panacea. The research emphasizes the need for a cultural shift in how society values women's work and addresses the structural barriers that limit their economic opportunities. Without this shift, efforts to close the gap will be incomplete and the cycle of economic inequality will continue.

Intersectionality: The Compounded Disadvantages Faced by Marginalized Women

While the gender wealth gap affects all women, its impact is not felt equally across different racial, ethnic, and socioeconomic groups. Intersectionality, the idea that multiple social identities intersect to create unique experiences of discrimination and disadvantage, is critical to understanding the full scope of the gender wealth gap. Women of color, LGBTQ+ women, and women from lower-income backgrounds often face compounded forms of discrimination that exacerbate their economic vulnerability (Kim et al., 2023). These women are more likely to be concentrated in low-paying, insecure jobs, and they often face additional barriers to accessing education, healthcare, and financial services, further widening the wealth gap.

The research highlights how the intersection of gender, race, and class creates unique economic challenges for marginalized women. For example, women of color are disproportionately represented in low-wage industries such as hospitality, retail, and domestic work, which offer little job security, few benefits, and limited opportunities for advancement. These women also face higher rates of workplace discrimination, including wage theft, harassment, and unequal pay compared to their white counterparts. The intersection of these multiple forms of discrimination creates a compounded disadvantage that makes it even more difficult for marginalized women to accumulate wealth and achieve financial independence (Kim et al., 2023).

LGBTQ+ women also face unique economic challenges, as they are often subject to both gender-based and sexuality-based discrimination in the labor market. Research suggests that LGBTQ+ women are more likely to experience wage discrimination, job insecurity, and barriers to career advancement compared to their heterosexual counterparts. These compounded forms of discrimination contribute to higher rates of poverty and financial insecurity among LGBTQ+ women, further widening the gender wealth gap.

Health Disparities and Economic Consequences: The Vicious Cycle of Inequality

Health disparities, particularly those related to gender and occupational class, further exacerbate the economic challenges faced by women, particularly those in lower-income jobs. Women in lower-status occupations are more likely to experience health problems such as musculoskeletal pain, psychological distress, and chronic illness, which can significantly impact their ability to work and earn a stable income (Nguyen et al., 2020). These health issues are often a result of physically demanding jobs, high levels of stress, and lack of access to adequate healthcare, all of which are more prevalent in low-paying industries where women are overrepresented.

The economic consequences of poor health are profound. Women who experience health problems are more likely to miss work, retire early, or be forced into part-time or precarious employment, all of which reduce their earning potential and limit their ability to accumulate wealth (Kjellsson, 2021). The financial burden of healthcare costs, coupled with lost wages due to illness or disability, creates a vicious cycle of economic disadvantage that is difficult to escape. Moreover, women in poor health may be less able to invest in their own education or career development, further limiting their opportunities for upward mobility and wealth accumulation (Nguyen et al., 2020).

The intersection of health disparities and economic inequality highlights the need for comprehensive policies that address both the social determinants of health and the structural barriers to economic equality. Ensuring that women have access to affordable healthcare, safe working conditions, and supportive workplace policies is critical to breaking the cycle of economic disadvantage and promoting long-term financial security.

A Call for Structural Change to Achieve Gender Equity

The gender wealth and pay gap is not merely an economic issue; it reflects broader societal inequalities that have deep roots in gender norms, discrimination, and structural barriers. Women's lower lifetime earnings, driven by career interruptions, part-time work, and occupational segregation, result in significant long-term financial insecurity, particularly in retirement. The broader economic consequences of these disparities extend beyond individual women, affecting families, communities, and the overall stability of society.

Despite policy efforts and corporate initiatives aimed at closing the gap, much more needs to be done to achieve true gender equity. Addressing the intersectionality of these issues is crucial (Kjellsson, 2021), particularly for marginalized women who face compounded forms of discrimination based on race, ethnicity, sexual orientation, and socioeconomic status. Achieving gender equity will require not only policy reforms but also a cultural shift in how society values women's work and addresses the structural barriers that limit their economic opportunities.

Ultimately, the gender wealth and pay gap is a systemic issue that requires a multifaceted approach to address its root causes. By promoting equal pay, providing better access to retirement savings and financial education, and addressing the social determinants of health and economic inequality, society can take meaningful steps toward achieving gender equity and ensuring that all women can build financial security and independence.

CHAPTER IX

THE ROLE OF POLICY AND LEGISLATION IN WOMEN'S ECONOMIC EMPOWERMENT

The role of policy and legislation in fostering women's economic empowerment cannot be understated. These frameworks act as foundational tools that either facilitate or inhibit women's full participation in the economy. Historically, women have been marginalized, excluded from economic activities due to institutional and legal constraints that reinforced gender inequality. Removing such barriers through robust policy interventions and progressive legislation is pivotal in ensuring women have equal opportunities in education, labor, property ownership, and leadership roles. Policies that guarantee women's rights—such as those promoting equal pay, prohibiting gender-based discrimination, and ensuring women's access to healthcare, education, and finance—are fundamental in driving economic growth and societal prosperity (Dahlum et al., 2022). It is not just about fairness; when women participate equally in the economy, it leads to a higher level of innovation, improved productivity, and overall economic benefits for the society at large. Enacting gender-sensitive laws thus becomes not just a moral imperative but an economic necessity (Misra et al., 2007). However, laws alone cannot be sufficient. These legal provisions must be actively enforced, and this enforcement should be coupled with efforts to change societal attitudes and eliminate cultural norms that perpetuate gender-based discrimination (Hainard & Verschuur, 2001).

Many countries have recognized the economic importance of including women in decision-making roles, leading to reforms in both policy and legislation. Yet, despite the progress made, deeply entrenched societal norms continue to pose challenges. In many parts of the world, women still face discrimination, exclusion from the workforce, and restrictions in accessing financial resources and property rights. Legal reforms must be accompanied by campaigns to change these outdated cultural norms, or the economic potential of half the population will remain underutilized (Banerjee & Gogoi, 2023). In particular, policies should not just focus on granting legal rights, but also ensuring that these rights are accessible and effectively realized in everyday life. This calls for an inclusive approach to economic planning, where women are considered in every facet of economic policy—be it taxation, employment regulations, or welfare systems (Dahlum et al., 2022).

Historical Context of Women's Economic Rights

Tracing the evolution of women's economic rights provides critical insights into how legal systems have both hindered and facilitated women's empowerment over time. In many societies, women historically faced rigid gender roles that confined them to domestic responsibilities, limiting their ability to own property, receive an education, or engage in formal employment. For instance, in Indonesia, the passage of the Marriage Law of 1974 was a landmark legal reform that granted women greater autonomy over their lives and economic choices. Prior to this law, women were subject to male guardianship in nearly all aspects of their personal and professional lives. The Marriage Law dismantled many of these barriers, allowing women the right to make independent decisions regarding employment, residence, and contracts—thereby paving the way for their increased participation in economic activities (Hidayah, 2023). This legal transformation continued with the introduction of gender-equal retirement ages, providing women with equal access to employment opportunities as their male counterparts.

Global perspectives further reveal significant milestones in the advancement of women's rights. For instance, landmark legislation such as the Equal Pay Act, enacted in several countries, aimed to close the wage gap between men and women. This legislation emerged after decades of women being paid less for performing the same work as men, reinforcing their secondary economic status (Misra et al., 2007). Similarly, Title IX of the United States Education Amendments of 1972 provided a platform for women to gain equal access to educational opportunities, which is an essential precursor to economic empowerment (Hainard & Verschuur, 2001). Access to education allowed more women to enter high-paying and high-status jobs, further driving economic growth. While some countries adopted gender-sensitive legislation earlier than others, the trend toward ensuring equal rights for women has been global, influenced by international conventions and agreements.

The trajectory of women's rights in Indonesia, like in many other regions, demonstrates that while progress has been made, it has not been without setbacks. From the mid-1970s to the mid-1990s, progress stagnated, highlighting that the implementation of legal reforms is often inconsistent, reflecting the broader societal and political challenges that may arise during certain periods. Yet, a resurgence in gender-sensitive legal reforms took place in the early 2000s, with the Labor Law of 2003 explicitly prohibiting gender-based discrimination in the workplace. This law opened up new avenues for women to engage in the workforce without fear of legal or social retribution (Hidayah, 2023). Such legislative strides illustrate the long and often winding path toward gender equality.

Landmark Legislation and Its Transformative Impact

Landmark legislation has served as a critical catalyst for women's economic participation, and its effects have been transformative both at national and global levels. In Indonesia, several key pieces of legislation, such as the 2004 Domestic Violence Law and the recent 2022 legislation protecting women from sexual harassment in the workplace, have provided women with the legal protections necessary to participate safely and fully in the economy (Hidayah, 2023). These laws not only protect women from violence but also contribute to creating an environment where women can engage in professional and economic activities without the fear of exploitation or abuse. Globally, laws such as the Equal Pay Act and Title IX have set legal precedents that have reshaped the economic landscape for women, particularly in areas such as education, employment, and property rights (Misra et al., 2007).

The importance of these legislative frameworks cannot be overemphasized. Without legal protections that ensure fair treatment and equal access to economic opportunities, women remain vulnerable to exploitation, underpayment, and exclusion from critical economic sectors. For example, the prohibition of gender-based discrimination in the workplace—enshrined in laws like the 2003 Labor Law in Indonesia—has been essential in breaking down barriers that prevented women from entering certain professions (Hidayah, 2023). Such laws, however, must be enforced rigorously, or their impact will remain symbolic rather than substantive. Moreover, policy interventions should also address issues such as occupational segregation, where women are disproportionately represented in lower-paying jobs, further perpetuating the gender wage gap (Banerjee & Gogoi, 2023).

The Role of International Organizations and Agreements

International organizations and global agreements have had a profound impact on the advancement of women's economic rights. International bodies such as the United Nations have been pivotal in advocating for gender equality and supporting the creation of global norms that prioritize women's economic empowerment. For instance, the UN's efforts through conventions like the Convention on the Elimination of All Forms of Discrimination Against Women (CEDAW) have pressured national governments to adopt gender-sensitive policies and legal frameworks (Dahlum et al., 2022). These international agreements set a global standard that encourages countries to adopt policies that promote women's economic participation.

Moreover, international organizations such as the World Bank have provided critical data on gender disparities in economic participation, helping to guide both international and national efforts toward achieving gender equality. Data-driven reports by the World Bank and other global institutions have highlighted the systemic discrimination women face in labor markets worldwide and have been instrumental in advocating for policy changes (Hainard & Verschuur, 2001). International collaboration through initiatives like Development Alternatives with Women for a New Era (DAWN) has also been influential in pushing for alternative development models that prioritize women's empowerment, particularly in the Global South. These initiatives ensure that women's voices are included in conversations around economic planning and that gender equality remains a priority in international development strategies.

The influence of international organizations is not limited to advocating for legal reforms; they also play a role in implementing programs that directly impact women's lives. For instance, international development programs aimed at increasing women's financial literacy and access to microfinance have been particularly successful in fostering economic independence for women in developing countries (Hidayah, 2023). These programs work hand-in-hand with legal reforms to create an ecosystem that supports women's full economic participation.

Policy Challenges and Opportunities

Despite the significant progress made through legal reforms and international advocacy, substantial challenges remain. Deep-seated societal norms and gender roles continue to act as barriers to women's economic empowerment. In many societies, women are still relegated to caregiving and domestic responsibilities, limiting their ability to engage fully in the workforce (Banerjee & Gogoi, 2023). Even where legal reforms have been implemented, these norms often prevent women from realizing their rights. For example, policies aimed at work-family reconciliation, such as paid maternity leave or flexible working hours, have been instrumental in supporting women's dual roles as caregivers and economic actors. Yet, despite these policies, women—particularly mothers—continue to face significant employment and earnings penalties. The "earner-carer" strategy, which promotes the idea that both men and women should share caregiving and employment responsibilities, has proven to be one of the more effective approaches in advancing gender equality (Misra et al., 2007). However, its success is contingent upon societal acceptance of shared caregiving responsibilities, a norm that is slow to change in many parts of the world.

Current policy challenges also include the persistent gender pay gap, occupational segregation, and limited access to financial resources and property. For women in many regions, particularly in the Global South, access to credit and financial services remains a significant barrier to entrepreneurship and economic participation (Hainard & Verschuur, 2001). Addressing these challenges requires a multifaceted approach that goes beyond legal reforms to include financial inclusion initiatives, education, and training programs, as well as societal awareness campaigns aimed at shifting cultural norms. Additionally, policymakers must ensure that legal frameworks are adaptive and responsive to new and emerging economic challenges, such as the rise of the digital economy, which presents both opportunities and risks for women's economic participation (Dahlum et al., 2022).

Legal reforms have been pivotal in removing barriers to women's economic participation, yet the realization of these rights remains uneven due to persistent societal norms and structural inequalities. The role of international organizations has been critical in advocating for gender-sensitive policies and promoting global standards for gender equality. However, much work remains to be done. Future policy efforts must focus not only on enacting laws but also on changing societal attitudes, improving financial inclusion, and ensuring that women can access the same opportunities as men in the evolving global economy. The transformation of women's economic roles requires a coordinated effort between governments, international organizations, and civil society to create an inclusive economic environment that allows women to fully realize their potential.

CHAPTER X

THE FUTURE OF WOMEN IN ECONOMICS

The role of women in economics has undergone substantial changes over the past few decades, driven by both necessity and ambition. This transformation has been most evident in developing countries, where women have increasingly taken on entrepreneurial roles as a way to lift their families out of poverty. In countries like Albania and India, where traditional gender norms often relegated women to the private sphere, economic necessity has become a powerful motivator for women to break free from these societal constraints (Arpita Singh & Ripudaman Singh, 2022). Despite this progress, however, deep-seated challenges continue to prevent women from fully realizing their economic potential. These challenges, which include limited access to financial resources, education, and social networks, are compounded by deeply ingrained patriarchal systems that are slow to evolve (Ahmetaj et al., 2023); (Andrew et al., 2024).

Globally, women entrepreneurs tend to operate out of necessity rather than opportunity. This trend is particularly evident in developing countries, where women are often the primary breadwinners of their households (Ahmetaj et al., 2023). In Albania, for example, a significant percentage of women start their own businesses due to limited opportunities in the formal labor market. This stands in stark contrast to high-income countries, where entrepreneurship is often driven by innovation and a desire to capitalize on emerging market opportunities (Arpita Singh & Ripudaman Singh, 2022). The reference texts suggest that while women in emerging economies are making strides in entrepreneurship, their success is often limited by systemic challenges, such as a lack of access to financial institutions that are necessary for scaling their businesses. In this context, it becomes clear that while progress is being made, the road to true economic equality remains long and difficult.

Moreover, the digital divide remains a significant barrier to women's economic advancement, particularly in developing economies. The rapid development of technology, while offering opportunities for economic growth and expansion, also poses risks for women who are disproportionately excluded from the digital economy. In Albania, for instance, women are underrepresented in the IT sector, which is rapidly becoming one of the most crucial areas for economic growth in the country (Ahmetaj et al., 2023). The lack of women in these fields highlights a broader issue of gender inequality in access to technology and education, which could prevent women from fully participating in future economic opportunities (Andrew et al., 2024). This digital divide is not only a problem in Albania but also in other parts of the world, where women are less likely to have access to the skills and resources necessary to thrive in a technology-driven economy.

Challenges in Women's Economic Participation: Systemic Barriers

Across different regions, the barriers that women face in economic participation are deeply rooted in systemic inequality. In both academia and the broader labor market, women continue to face discrimination that limits their access to leadership positions. In the field of economics, for example, women are underrepresented in key decision-making roles, which limits their ability to influence important economic policies (Lundberg & Stearns, 2019). This underrepresentation is significant not only for the individuals involved but also for society as a whole, as it perpetuates a cycle in which women's perspectives and experiences are systematically excluded from the policy-making process. The failure to incorporate diverse viewpoints into economic decision-making can have broad implications, particularly when it comes to addressing issues like gender inequality and economic development (Andrew et al., 2024).

Further complicating the issue is the fact that women, particularly in emerging economies, often lack access to the financial resources necessary to grow their businesses (Ahmetaj et al., 2023). In countries like Albania, women entrepreneurs frequently face difficulties in securing loans, as financial institutions often view them as higher-risk clients due to deeply ingrained gender biases. This lack of access to financing is one of the primary reasons why women-led businesses often remain small and underdeveloped, despite their potential to contribute significantly to the economy (Arpita Singh & Ripudaman Singh, 2022). This issue is not limited to Albania or India; globally, women entrepreneurs face similar challenges, particularly in sectors that are dominated by men, such as technology and finance.

The research also underscores how deeply entrenched patriarchal norms continue to affect women's economic participation (Lundberg & Stearns, 2019). In many societies, women are expected to prioritize their roles as caregivers and homemakers, which limits their ability to engage in full-time work or pursue entrepreneurial ventures. This expectation is particularly pronounced in emerging economies, where traditional gender roles are more rigidly enforced (Ahmetaj et al., 2023). Even in more developed countries, where gender norms are ostensibly more progressive, women continue to shoulder a disproportionate amount of domestic labor, which limits their career advancement. These societal expectations not only hinder women's economic participation but also reinforce the gender wage gap, as women are more likely to work part-time or take career breaks to care for children or elderly relatives (Andrew et al., 2024).

The Role of Technology in Women's Economic Futures

Technology is one of the most significant drivers of change in the global economy, and its impact on women's economic futures cannot be overstated. On one hand, technology offers unprecedented opportunities for women to break into new fields and scale their businesses. Digital platforms, for example, have enabled women entrepreneurs to reach global markets in ways that were previously unimaginable (Ahmetaj et al., 2023). This is particularly true in sectors like e-commerce and digital marketing, where women have been able to leverage technology to grow their businesses despite facing barriers in more traditional sectors (Andrew et al., 2024). In this sense, technology can serve as an equalizer, allowing women to bypass some of the systemic barriers that have historically limited their economic participation (Arpita Singh & Ripudaman Singh, 2022).

However, technology also poses significant risks for women, particularly in terms of the digital divide (Ahmetaj et al., 2023). In many parts of the world, women have less access to the internet and digital devices than men, which limits their ability to participate in the digital economy. This issue is particularly pronounced in developing countries like Albania, where women are underrepresented in the IT sector and lack access to the digital skills necessary to compete in the global economy. The reference texts highlight that addressing this digital divide will be crucial if women are to fully benefit from the opportunities presented by technological advancements (Andrew et al., 2024). Moreover, even in countries where women have access to technology, they are often excluded from leadership roles in tech-related fields, which limits their ability to influence the direction of technological innovation (Lundberg & Stearns, 2019).

In addition to the digital divide, automation and artificial intelligence (AI) represent both a challenge and an opportunity for women. On the one hand, these technologies have the potential to disrupt labor markets by displacing jobs that are traditionally held by women, such as those in the service and care sectors (Andrew et al., 2024). On the other hand, automation and AI could create new opportunities for women in fields like data analysis and software development, provided that they have access to the education and training needed to take advantage of these opportunities (Ahmetaj et al., 2023). The reference texts suggest that the key to ensuring that women benefit from these technological changes will be to invest in education and skills development, particularly in STEM fields, where women are currently underrepresented.

Strategies for Sustaining Women's Economic Empowerment

To ensure that the progress made by women in economics is sustained, a comprehensive, multi-faceted approach is needed. This approach must address the systemic barriers that women face, including access to financial resources, education, and social networks (Ahmetaj et al., 2023). Governments and institutions must continue to implement policies that support women entrepreneurs, such as offering microfinance programs that provide women with the capital they need to start and grow their businesses. Moreover, efforts must be made to challenge and change the patriarchal norms that limit women's economic participation (Lundberg & Stearns, 2019). This will require a concerted effort not only from policymakers but also from communities and families, who must work to create an environment in which women are encouraged to pursue their economic goals (Andrew et al., 2024).

In terms of education, the reference texts emphasize the importance of providing women with access to both formal education and vocational training. This is particularly important in emerging economies, where women are often excluded from higher education due to financial constraints or societal expectations (Ahmetaj et al., 2023). In India, for example, the government has implemented several programs aimed at increasing women's access to education, particularly in rural areas where traditional gender norms are more pronounced (Arpita Singh & Ripudaman Singh, 2022). These programs have been successful in increasing the number of women entrepreneurs, but more work needs to be done to ensure that women have access to the training and mentorship needed to succeed in male-dominated sectors like technology and finance.

Mentorship and networking programs are also essential components of a strategy to sustain women's economic empowerment (Lundberg & Stearns, 2019). Women entrepreneurs often lack access to the social networks that are necessary for business success, which limits their ability to secure financing, build partnerships, and access markets (Ahmetaj et al., 2023). Mentorship programs that connect women with experienced entrepreneurs and business leaders can help to bridge this gap and provide women with the support they need to succeed. These programs are particularly important in fields like technology, where women are underrepresented and often lack the mentorship needed to advance in their careers (Andrew et al., 2024).

The progress that has been made in increasing women's participation in entrepreneurship and the broader labor market must be supported by policies and programs that address the systemic barriers that women continue to face (Ahmetaj et al., 2023). At the same time, efforts must be made to ensure that women have access to the education and resources needed to thrive in a rapidly changing global economy (Andrew et al., 2024). With the right policies and support systems in place, women have the potential to play an increasingly important role in shaping the future of the global economy, driving innovation, and contributing to economic growth (Lundberg & Stearns, 2019).

References

1. Ahmetaj, B., Kruja, A. D., & Hysa, E. (2023). Women Entrepreneurship: Challenges and Perspectives of an Emerging Economy. Administrative Sciences, 13(4), 111. https://doi.org/10.3390/admsci13040111
2. Anderson, A., Chilczuk, S., Nelson, K., Ruther, R., & Wall-Scheffler, C. (2023). The Myth of Man the Hunter: Women's contribution to the hunt across ethnographic contexts. PLOS ONE, 18(6), e0287101. https://doi.org/10.1371/journal.pone.0287101
3. Andrew, A., Bandiera, O., Costa Dias, M., & Landais, C. (2024). Women and men at work. Oxford Open Economics, 3(Supplement_1), i294–i322. https://doi.org/10.1093/ooec/odad034
4. Andrews, C. (2022). Feminism and the Mexican Revolution. SUURJ: Seattle University Undergraduate Research Journal, 6.
5. Arpita Singh & Ripudaman Singh. (2022). Women Entrepreneurs in India: Evolution, Current Challenges and Future Prospects. Journal of Pharmaceutical Negative Results, 13(4), 729–735. https://doi.org/10.47750/pnr.2022.13.04.098
6. Banerjee, S., & Gogoi, P. (2023). Exploring the role of financial empowerment in mitigating the gender differentials in subjective and objective health outcomes among the older population in India. PLOS ONE, 18(1), e0280887. https://doi.org/10.1371/journal.pone.0280887
7. Cashdan, L. (1989). Anti-war feminism: New directions, new dualities—a Marxist-humanist perspective. Women's Studies International Forum, 12(1), 81–85. https://doi.org/10.1016/0277-5395(89)90083-6
8. Cohen, M. (n.d.). CHANGING PERCEPTIONS OF THE IMPACT OF THE INDUSTRIAL REVOLUTION ON FEMALE LABOUR.
9. Cowan, R. S. (1976). The "Industrial Revolution" in the Home: Household Technology and Social Change in the 20th Century. Technology and Culture, 17(1), 1. https://doi.org/10.2307/3103251
10. Dahlum, S., Knutsen, C. H., & Mechkova, V. (2022). Women's political empowerment and economic growth. World Development, 156, 105822. https://doi.org/10.1016/j.worlddev.2022.105822
11. Duflo, E. (2012). Women Empowerment and Economic Development. Journal of Economic Literature, 50(4), 1051–1079.

12. Evans, S. M. (2015). Women's Liberation: Seeing the Revolution Clearly. Feminist Studies, 41(1)
13. Fedurek, P., Lacroix, L., Lehmann, J., Aktipis, A., Cronk, L., Townsend, C., Makambi, E. J., Mabulla, I., Behrends, V., & Berbesque, J. C. (2020). Status does not predict stress: Women in an egalitarian hunter–gatherer society. Evolutionary Human Sciences, 2, e44. https://doi.org/10.1017/ehs.2020.44
14. Foster, J. B., & Clark, B. (2018). Women, Nature, and Capital in the Industrial Revolution. Monthly Review, 1–24. https://doi.org/10.14452/MR-069-08-2018-01_1
15. Goldin, C. D. (1991). The_role_of_world_war_ii_in_the_rise_of_womens_employment.pdf. 81(4), 741–756.
16. Gonçalves, T. C., Gaio, C., & Rodrigues, M. (2022). The Impact of Women Power on Firm Value. Administrative Sciences, 12(3), 93. https://doi.org/10.3390/admsci12030093
17. Hainard, F., & Verschuur, C. (2001). Filling the Urban Policy Breach: Women's Empowerment, Grass-Roots Organizations, and Urban Governance. International Political Science Review / Revue Internationale de Science Politique, 22(1,), 33–53.
18. Hansen, C. W., Jensen, P. S., & Skovsgaard, C. V. (2015). Modern gender roles and agricultural history: The Neolithic inheritance. Journal of Economic Growth, 20(4), 365–404. https://doi.org/10.1007/s10887-015-9119-yHidayah, N. (2023). Gender, Economy, and the Law: Women Entrepreneurs in Indonesian and Islamic Legal Perspectives. Samarah: Jurnal Hukum Keluarga Dan Hukum Islam, 7(2), 1171. https://doi.org/10.22373/sjhk.v7i2.17944
19. Islam, M. (2011). Third World Women in the Development Process: Feminist Thoughts and Debates.
20. Jaworski, T. (2014). "You're in the Army Now:" The Impact of World War II on Women's Education, Work, and Family. The Journal of Economic History, 74(1), 169–195. https://doi.org/10.1017/S0022050714000060
21. Johnson, A. (2018). The War to End All Wars on Ideal Female Figures: An Analysis of WWI and its Effects on U.S. Women's Fashion from 1917-1927. 7(3).
22. Kim, M., Chen, J. J., & Weinberg, B. A. (2023). Gender pay gaps in economics: A deeper look at institutional factors. Agricultural

Economics, 54(4), 471–486. https://doi.org/10.1111/agec.12778

23. Kjellsson, S. (2021). Do working conditions contribute differently to gender gaps in self-rated health within different occupational classes? Evidence from the Swedish Level of Living Survey. PLOS ONE, 16(6), e0253119. https://doi.org/10.1371/journal.pone.0253119
24. Licumba, E. A., Dzator, J., & Zhang, X. (2016). Health and economic growth: Are there gendered effects?: Evidence from selected southern Africa development community region. The Journal of Developing Areas, 50(5), 215–227. https://doi.org/10.1353/jda.2016.0056
25. Litman, L., Robinson, J., Rosen, Z., Rosenzweig, C., Waxman, J., & Bates, L. M. (2020). The persistence of pay inequality: The gender pay gap in an anonymous online labor market. PLOS ONE, 15(2), e0229383. https://doi.org/10.1371/journal.pone.0229383
26. Lundberg, S., & Stearns, J. (2019). Women in Economics: Stalled Progress. Journal of Economic Perspectives, 33(1), 3–22. https://doi.org/10.1257/jep.33.1.3
27. Mauconduit, N., Emile, E. S., & Paul, B. (2013). Women and economic development: Women entrepreneurship situation in Haiti. 2(3).
28. Meriküll, J., Meriküll, J., Kukk, M., & Rõõm, T. (2021). What explains the gender gap in wealth? Evidence from administrative data. 19, 501–547.
29. Miller, G. (2008). Women's Suffrage, Political Responsiveness, and Child Survival in American History *. Quarterly Journal of Economics, 123(3), 1287–1327. https://doi.org/10.1162/qjec.2008.123.3.1287
30. Misra, J., Budig, M. J., & Moller, S. (2007). Reconciliation policies and the effects of motherhood on employment, earnings and poverty. Journal of Comparative Policy Analysis: Research and Practice, 9(2), 135–155. https://doi.org/10.1080/13876980701311588
31. Nguyen, T. T., Darnell, A., Weissman, A., Frongillo, E. A., Mathisen, R., Lapping, K., Mastro, T. D., & Withers, M. (2020). Social, economic, and political events affect gender equity in China, Nepal, and Nicaragua: A matched, interrupted time-series study. Global Health Action, 13(1), 1712147. https://doi.org/10.1080/16549716.2020.1712147
32. Ojediran, F. (Olufunmilola), & Anderson, A. (2020). Women's Entrepreneurship in the Global South: Empowering and Emancipating? Administrative Sciences, 10(4), 87. https://doi.org/10.3390/admsci10040087
33. Pierli, G., Murmura, F., & Palazzi, F. (2022). Women and Leadership: How Do Women Leaders Contribute to Companies' Sustainable

Choices? Frontiers in Sustainability, 3, 930116. https://doi.org/10.3389/frsus.2022.930116

34. Redd, D. A. (1998). The Hadza and Kaguru of Tanzania: Gender roles and privileges at two subsistence levels.
35. Shatnawi, D., & Fishback, P. (2018). The Impact of World War II on the Demand for Female Workers in Manufacturing. The Journal of Economic History, 78(2), 539–574. https://doi.org/10.1017/S0022050718000232
36. Stanfors, M., & Goldscheider, F. (2017). The forest and the trees: Industrialization, demographic change, and the ongoing gender revolution in Sweden and the United States, 1870-2010. Demographic Research, 36, 173–226. https://doi.org/10.4054/DemRes.2017.36.6
37. Stromquist, N. P. (2015). Explaining the expansion of feminist ideas: Cultural diffusion or political struggle? Globalisation, Societies and Education, 13(1), 109–134. https://doi.org/10.1080/14767724.2014.967489
38. Subrahmanian, M. (2019). Autonomous Women's Movement in Kerala: Historiography. 20(2).
39. Testy, K. Y. (2019). From Governess to Governance: Advancing Gender Equity in Corporate Leadership. THE GEORGE WASHINGTON LAW REVIEW, 87.
40. Vellacott, J. (1987). Feminist Consciousness and the First World War. History Workshop Journal.
41. Walker, N. (1985). Humor and Gender Roles: The "Funny" Feminism of the Post-World War II Suburbs. American Quarterly, 37(1), 98. https://doi.org/10.2307/2712765
42. Zhang, Y., & Yu, Y. (2020). Women and the Leadership Role in Today's Workplace. 2(6).

www.ingramcontent.com/pod-product-compliance
Lightning Source LLC
LaVergne TN
LVHW040912150826
845672LV00007B/2002

* 9 7 9 8 8 9 6 3 2 2 4 6 7 *